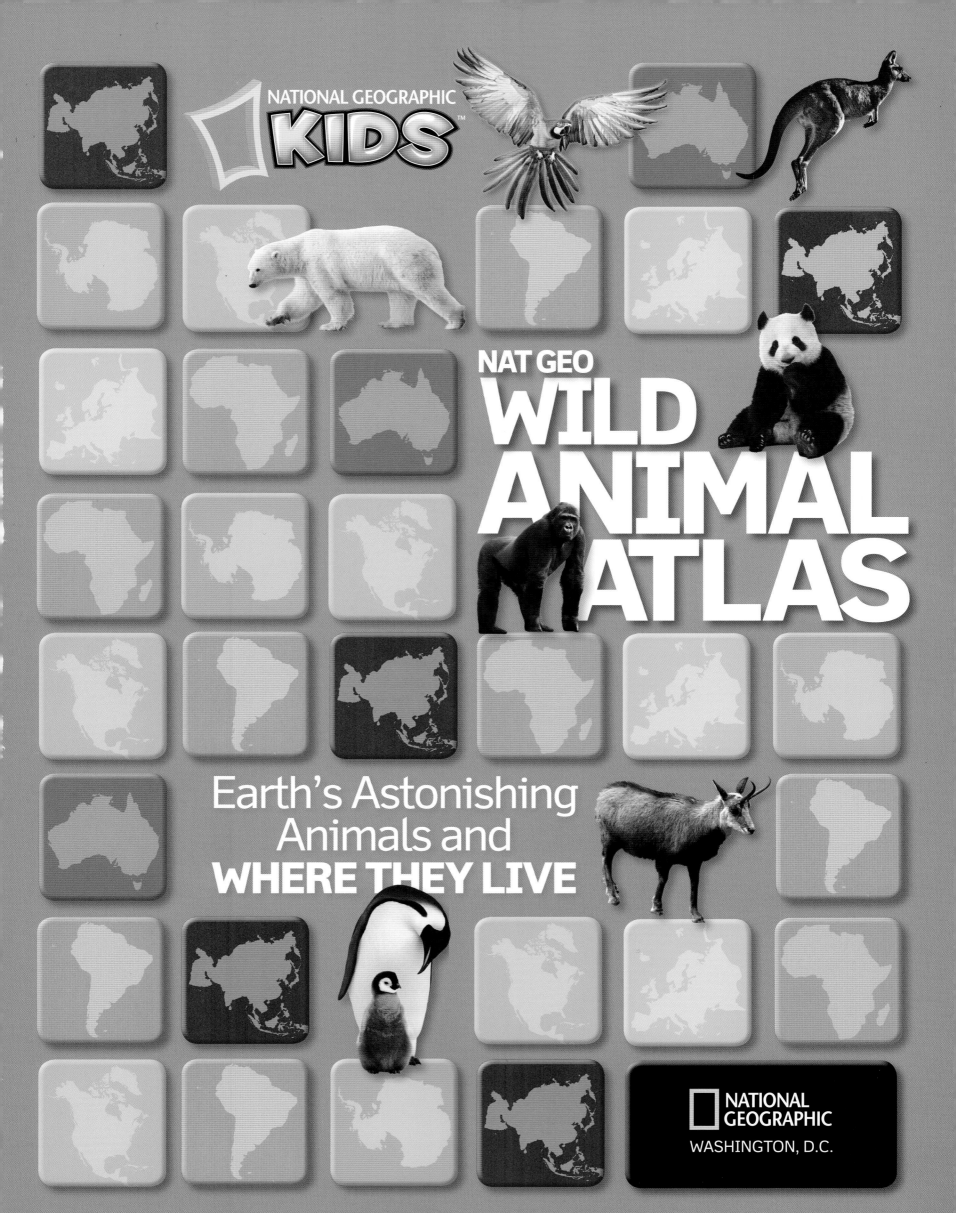

NATIONAL GEOGRAPHIC
KIDS™

NAT GEO
WILD
ANIMAL
ATLAS

Earth's Astonishing
Animals and
WHERE THEY LIVE

NATIONAL
GEOGRAPHIC
WASHINGTON, D.C.

CONTENTS

NOTE: The animals included in this book are not shown to scale.

ASIA
32

AFRICA
40

AUSTRALIA
48

ANTARCTICA
56

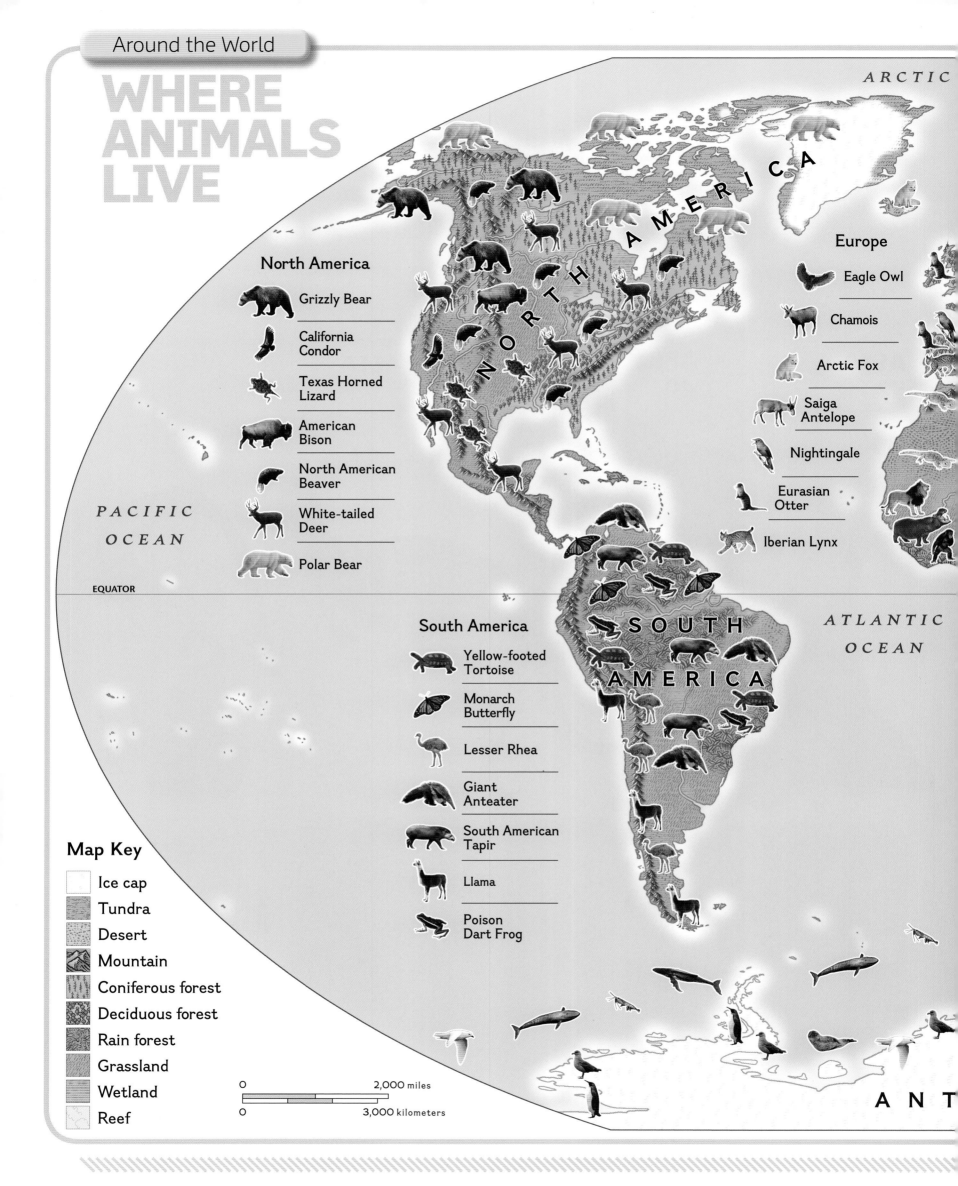

WHERE ANIMALS LIVE

ARCTIC

NORTH AMERICA

North America

- Grizzly Bear
- California Condor
- Texas Horned Lizard
- American Bison
- North American Beaver
- White-tailed Deer
- Polar Bear

PACIFIC OCEAN

EQUATOR

Europe

- Eagle Owl
- Chamois
- Arctic Fox
- Saiga Antelope
- Nightingale
- Eurasian Otter
- Iberian Lynx

SOUTH AMERICA

ATLANTIC OCEAN

South America

- Yellow-footed Tortoise
- Monarch Butterfly
- Lesser Rhea
- Giant Anteater
- South American Tapir
- Llama
- Poison Dart Frog

Map Key

- Ice cap
- Tundra
- Desert
- Mountain
- Coniferous forest
- Deciduous forest
- Rain forest
- Grassland
- Wetland
- Reef

0	2,000 miles
0	3,000 kilometers

ANT

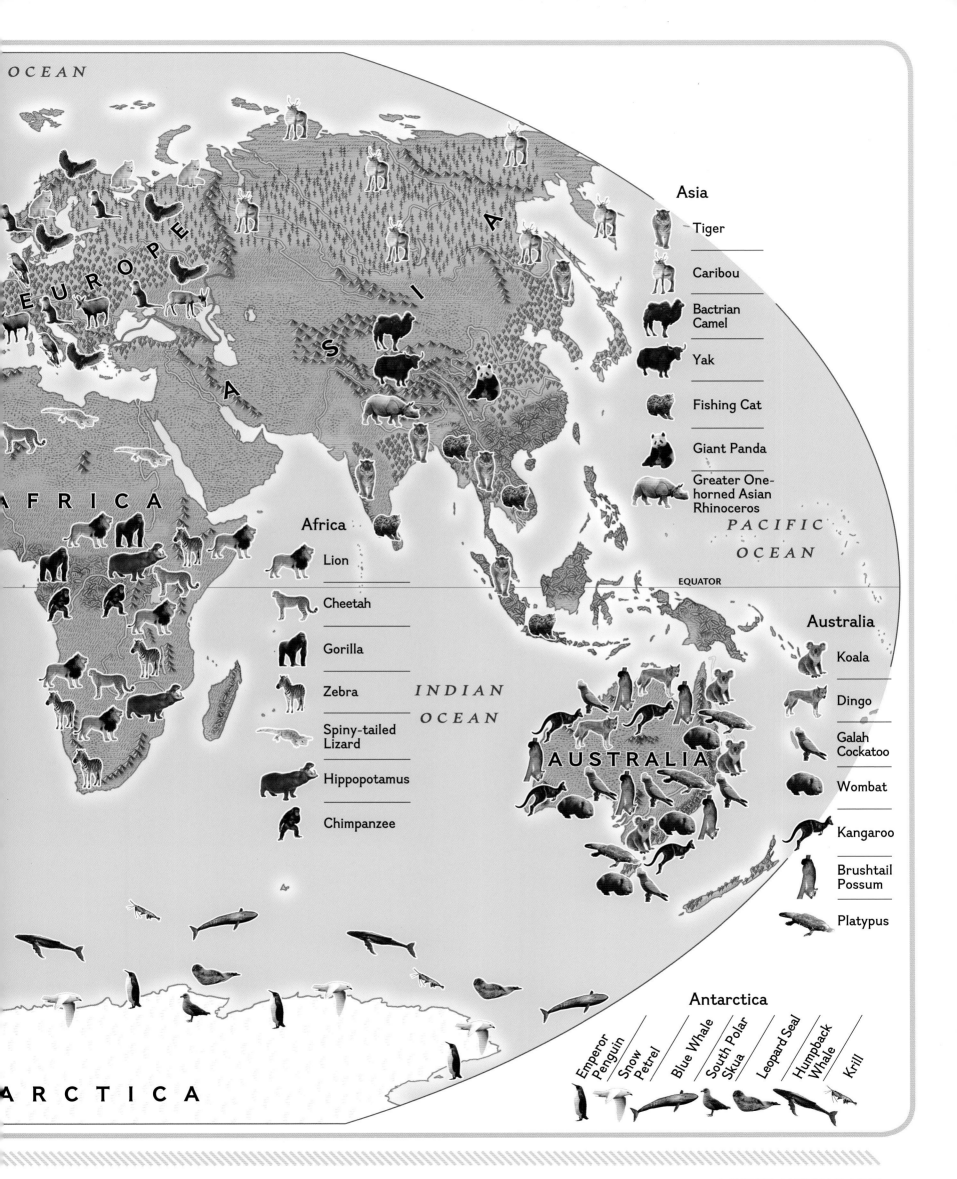

OCEAN

EUROPE

ASIA

AFRICA

PACIFIC OCEAN

EQUATOR

INDIAN OCEAN

AUSTRALIA

ARCTICA

Asia
Tiger

Caribou

Bactrian Camel

Yak

Fishing Cat

Giant Panda

Greater One-horned Asian Rhinoceros

Africa
Lion

Cheetah

Gorilla

Zebra

Spiny-tailed Lizard

Hippopotamus

Chimpanzee

Australia
Koala

Dingo

Galah Cockatoo

Wombat

Kangaroo

Brushtail Possum

Platypus

Antarctica
Emperor Penguin

Snow Petrel

Blue Whale

South Polar Skua

Leopard Seal

Humpback Whale

Krill

ANIMAL ECOSYSTEMS

Earth is made up of many different ecosystems. An ecosystem is a special community of plants and animals that depend on each other. Below are examples of some of Earth's main ecosystems.

ICE CAP This ecosystem, near Earth's poles, is always cold. Only animals that have adapted, such as these **King Penguins** in Antarctica, can survive this icy environment.

TUNDRA Found on high mountains and near Earth's polar regions, this cold ecosystem has only very short summers. Animals such as the **Caribou** live in this harsh region.

DESERT This dry ecosystem sometimes goes for years without rainfall. Animals such as this **Woma Python** near Ayers Rock in Australia survive with very little water.

MOUNTAIN The rocky landscape of this ecosystem is very challenging. Special hooves help animals such as these **Ibex** in the Italian Alps move quickly over the steep slopes.

FOREST Trees make up this ecosystem. Forests near the Equator, called rain forests, have many colorful birds, such as this **Scarlet Macaw** in the Amazon River Basin.

GRASSLAND Grasses, tall and short, make up this ecosystem. **Elephants,** such as these in Kenya's Masai Mara Reserve, are found in regions of tall tropical grasses called savanna.

WETLAND This ecosystem, which includes swamps and marshes, is covered with water at least part of each year. It is home to many animals, including this family of **Roe Deer**.

CORAL REEF Colorful fish swim through Australia's Great Barrier Reef. This ecosystem is made up of millions of skeletons of tiny sea creatures, such as these **Stony Corals.**

ICE CAP

MOUNTAIN

GRASSLAND

DESERT

TUNDRA

FOREST

WETLAND

CORAL REEF

ANIMAL BITES

DESPITE THEIR
IMPRESSIVE SIZE,
GRIZZLIES
ARE QUITE **FAST**
AND HAVE
BEEN CLOCKED AT
30 MILES
(48 KILOMETERS)
AN HOUR.

NORTH AMERICA

North America is 9,449,000 square miles (24,474,000 square kilometers) in area. It is the third largest continent and makes up almost 17 percent of Earth's land area. It stretches from ice caps and tundra in the north to tropical forests in the south with grasslands, wetlands, mountains, and deserts in between. These ecosystems are home to many animals, including this Grizzly Bear trying to catch a salmon in a river in Alaska.

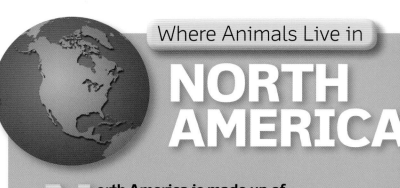

Where Animals Live in
NORTH AMERICA

California Condor

Texas Horned Lizard

American Bison

North American Beaver

White-tailed Deer

Polar Bear

ASIA

PACIFIC OCEAN

North America is made up of many different ecosystems. Each community of plants and animals represents special adaptation to its environment. Thousands of different animals live on the land, in the skies, or in the waters of the continent.

ICE CAP/TUNDRA This frozen region is home to many Arctic animals, including the Polar Bear. This giant mammal hunts seals in the icy waters of the north. Rising ocean temperatures and melting ice may put polar bears at risk by disrupting their food supply.

DESERT The Texas Horned Lizard is a fierce-looking member of the reptile family with numerous "horns" on its head and back. It eats mainly insects and lives in burrows in dry regions with very little vegetation.

MOUNTAIN California Condors live in rocky cliffs in the western mountains of North America. These huge birds can fly as high as 15,000 feet (4,572 meters). Condors are nature's housekeepers because they eat dead animals. Condors are an endangered species.

FOREST White-tailed Deer live mainly in forests and meadows of North America. The male deer, called a buck, can be identified by its antlers. White-tailed deer graze mainly at dawn or dusk and eat leaves, grasses, and twigs.

GRASSLAND Much of central North America is grassland, where animals such as the American Bison graze in herds. Bison were hunted almost to extinction in the 1800s.

WETLAND The North American Beaver, North America's largest rodent, is found throughout the region. Beavers are skilled engineers. They build dams out of mud, stones, and sticks in rivers and ponds.

Map Key

- ☐ Ice cap
- ▦ Tundra
- ▦ Desert
- ▲ Mountain
- ▦ Coniferous forest
- ▦ Deciduous forest
- ▦ Rain forest
- ▦ Grassland
- ▦ Wetland

ARCTIC
OCEAN

Greenland

Iceland
(EUROPE)

Alaska

ROCKY MOUNTAINS

CANADIAN SHIELD

GREAT PLAINS

Hudson
Bay

ATLANTIC
OCEAN

Sierra Nevada

Appalachian Mountains

Gulf
of
Mexico

W E S T   I N D I E S

Caribbean
Sea

Central America

Red dot indicates
an animal at risk.*

Grizzly Bear

California
Condor

Texas Horned
Lizard

American
Bison

North American
Beaver

White-tailed
Deer

Polar Bear

*Animals that are at
risk are in danger of
no longer being found
in the wild because
of loss of habitat or
danger from humans.

SOUTH AMERICA

0   500 miles

0   750 kilometers

THE SONORAN DESERT

The Sonoran Desert covers 120,000 square miles (310,799 square kilometers) in the southwestern United States and northwestern Mexico. It is the hottest North American desert, but seasonal rains support a wide variety of plant and animal life.

UNITED STATES

Sonoran Desert

MEXICO

PACIFIC OCEAN

0   200 miles
0   200 kilometers

2.52

0.52 0.51 0.67 0.23 0.12 0.33   1.61   1.12 1.10 0.85 0.89

JAN FEB MAR APR MAY JUN JUL AUG SEP OCT NOV DEC
Average inches of rainfall per month

RAINFALL IN THE SONORAN DESERT

GILA WOODPECKER
This bird often nests in a hole made with its sharp beak in a Saguaro cactus.

WESTERN DIAMONDBACK RATTLESNAKE
The Western Diamondback is the largest rattler living in the Sonoran Desert. Its venom can be deadly.

BANDED GILA MONSTER
This desert reptile is one of just two poisonous lizards found in North America.

Animal at risk

TURKEY VULTURE

These birds, with a wingspan of 6 feet (almost 2 meters), feed mainly on dead animals.

ANIMAL BITES

WHEN FLOWERS ARE IN BLOOM IN THE SONORAN DESERT, **BEES & BIRDS** POLLINATE THEM DURING THE DAY. AT NIGHT, **BATS** TAKE OVER THE JOB.

DESERT BIGHORN SHEEP

Desert bighorns have padded hooves that enable them to move quickly over steep, rocky terrain.

SONORAN PRONGHORN

Sharp eyesight and great speed protect this endangered animal from desert predators such as wolves.

BOBCAT

These felines live throughout North America, including desert areas. Because they hunt at night, bobcats are rarely seen.

GREATER ROADRUNNER

This desert bird rarely flies, but can run as fast as 15 miles (24 kilometers) an hour.

ANIMAL BITES

THE AMERICAN BISON IS
SO WELL INSULATED BY ITS
THICK SHAGGY COAT
THAT **SNOW**
CAN SETTLE ON ITS BACK
**WITHOUT
MELTING.**

Spotlight on

AMERICAN BISON

A bison calf stays close to its mother. Calves weigh 30 to 70 pounds (14 to 32 kilograms) at birth.

The American bison is a symbol of North America's frontier history. As many as 60 million bison may have roamed the grasslands of the Great Plains when Europeans first arrived. Most of the bison we see today are a product of breeding managed by conservationists. Although sometimes mistakenly called a buffalo, the bison is actually a relative of cattle and goats. Bison are the heaviest land animals in North America. They are considered to be more dangerous than a grizzly bear because they sometimes attack for no apparent reason, using their horns, their large skull, and their hind legs as deadly weapons.

Snow clings to a bison's face in Yellowstone National Park. The animal's shaggy hair protects it from the bitter cold of winter.

HABITAT Bison once roamed the grasslands of the Great Plains where they were an important part of the Plains Indian culture. Today most bison are found on ranches or in game preserves where they are raised for their meat.

DIET Bison are herbivores, meaning they eat only plant material. Their diet includes grasses, herbs, shrubs, and twigs. Like cattle, bison graze and then settle down to chew their food, which is stored in a special stomach.

SURVIVAL In the 1800s, bison were hunted almost to extinction. By careful breeding and protection on ranches and preserves, the number of bison in North America is now about 200,000.

FACTS AT A GLANCE

HABITAT Once found throughout the Great Plains of North America; now found on ranches and preserves

LIFESPAN An average of 12 to 20 years in the wild

SIZE 900 to 2,200 pounds (408 to 998 kilograms)

DIET Grasses, herbs, shrubs, twigs

Despite their huge size, bison can change directions quickly and run at speeds up to 35 miles (56 kilometers) an hour.

SOUTH AMERICA

South America is 6,880,000 square miles (17,819,000 square kilometers) in area. It is the fourth largest continent and makes up 12 percent of Earth's land area. Tropical rain forests in the north are drained by the mighty Amazon River. Snow-capped mountains form a western spine. And winds sweep across southern plateaus. These ecosystems are home to many animals, including this South American Yellow-footed Tortoise that eats flowers, fruits, and insects in tropical forests.

ANIMAL BITES

TORTOISES HAVE LIVED ON **EARTH** FOR ABOUT **230 MILLION YEARS,** SINCE THE BEGINNING OF THE AGE OF THE DINOSAURS.

SOUTH AMERICA

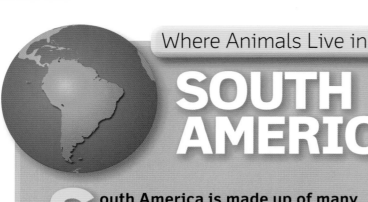

South America is made up of many different ecosystems. Thousands of animals, birds, and fish live in the many environments—on the land, in the skies, or in the waters—of this continent.

DESERT The Lesser Rhea does not fly, but can run up to 37 miles (60 kilometers) an hour. These large birds live in herds of 5 to 30 individuals. They feed on plants and small animals.

MOUNTAIN Sure-footed Llamas are used by peoples in the Andes Mountains as pack animals on the rugged mountain terrain. Relatives of the camel, they are known to kick or even spit when tired.

FOREST Poison Dart Frogs, one of the most toxic animals on Earth, and bright colored butterflies, like the Monarch, are just two of the unique creatures living in South America's rain forests. Scientists believe the vivid colors that make these creatures so beautiful may protect them by frightening away predators.

GRASSLAND Giant Anteaters use their tongues—more than 2 feet (0.6 meters) long—to catch insects. Anteaters live in grasslands and rain forests where they feast on as many as 35,000 ants and termites daily.

WETLAND The swamps and streams of this continent are home to the South American Tapir. A relative of the horse, tapirs use their trunk-like snouts to pull up grasses and aquatic plants.

Monarch Butterfly

Lesser Rhea

Giant Anteater

South American Tapir

Llama

Poison Dart Frog

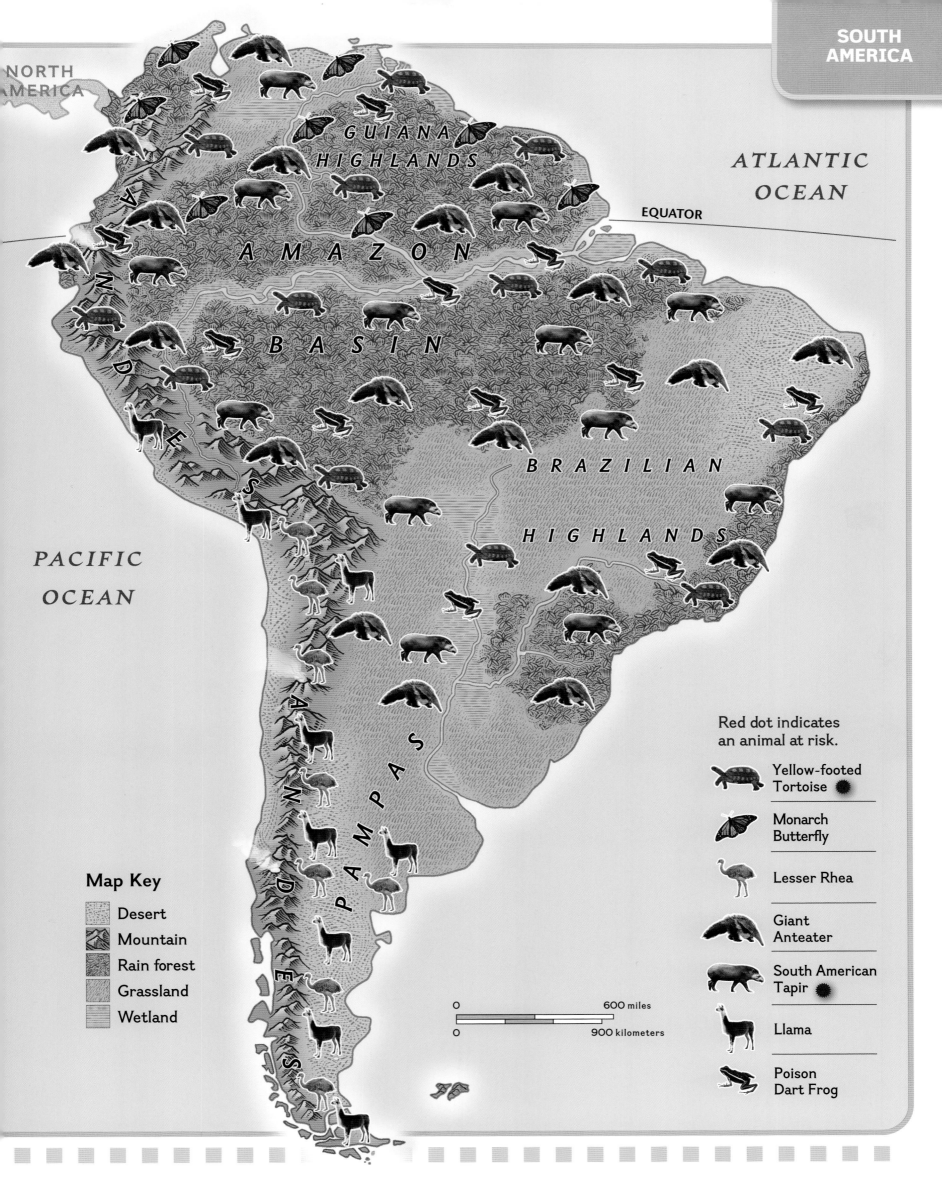

NORTH
AMERICA

ATLANTIC
OCEAN

GUIANA
HIGHLANDS

EQUATOR

A M A Z O N

B A S I N

A
N
D
E
S

PACIFIC
OCEAN

B R A Z I L I A N

H I G H L A N D S

P
A
M
P
A
S

A
N
D
E
S

Red dot indicates
an animal at risk.

Yellow-footed
Tortoise ●

Monarch
Butterfly

Lesser Rhea

Giant
Anteater

South American
Tapir ●

Llama

Poison
Dart Frog

Map Key

Desert

Mountain

Rain forest

Grassland

Wetland

0   600 miles

0   900 kilometers

THE AMAZON RAIN FOREST

The Amazon River basin includes Earth's largest rain forest. The rain forest covers an area almost the size of the 48 contiguous United States. Cutting down trees has put many rain forest animals at risk.

ATLANTIC OCEAN

Amazon Rain Forest

SOUTH AMERICA

0   1,000 miles

0   1,000 kilometers

Emergent layer
Up to 270 feet (82 m)

Canopy
65 to 130 feet
(20 to 40 m)

Understory
12 to 15 feet
(3 to 4 m)

Shrub layer

Forest floor

LAYERS OF THE AMAZON RAIN FOREST

Animal at risk

ANIMAL BITES

THE AMAZON RAIN FOREST PRODUCES ABOUT

20 PERCENT
OF EARTH'S
OXYGEN.

GOLDEN LION TAMARIN
These small orange-yellow monkeys eat fruits, insects, and lizards. They are almost extinct in the wild.

GREEN ANACONDA
This powerful snake is the largest on Earth. It kills its prey by squeezing it to death.

SPOTTED JAGUAR
Jaguars are the third largest member of the cat family. They live near water in the dense forest.

BLUE-AND-YELLOW MACAW
This brilliant blue and orange bird—popular as a pet—uses its strong beak to crack nuts and even coconuts.

THREE-TOED SLOTH
These sloths live in the treetops of the rain forest where they eat a diet of leaves and fruit.

PINK-TOED TARANTULA
Dark, hairy legs make this spider scary to see, but its venom is weak and harmless to humans.

RED-BELLIED PIRANHA
This freshwater fish uses sharp teeth to consume meat. It does not aggressively attack humans, as sometimes reported.

CAIMAN
A member of the alligator family, caimans live in wetlands where they eat fish, reptiles, and birds.

POISON DART FROGS

More than 300 different species of tree frogs live in Earth's tropical forests, but the greatest number are found in South America. They all have strong back legs that help them jump long distances. They also have special sticky pads on the tip of each toe. This makes it possible for them to move about on the undersides of leaves without falling to the forest floor far below. Most other tree frogs are green, brown, or gray. This helps them blend into the foliage of the forest. But poison dart frogs have bright-colored markings that scientists believe may frighten away predators. Three species of poison dart frogs are poisonous to humans. They have one of Earth's deadliest venoms found in their skin.

Poison dart frogs display a wide range of colors and markings, which may be a signal to predators to stay away.

ATLANTIC OCEAN

PACIFIC OCEAN

Poison dart frog range

SOUTH AMERICA

0   1,000 miles

0   1,000 kilometers

HABITAT Tree frogs are found in the warm tropics around the world. As the name suggests, they live high above the forest floor among the leaves of tall rain forest trees.

DIET Most tree frogs hunt at night and live on a diet of bugs, flies, moths, and other small creatures that live in the forest. Tree frogs catch their food with a fast flick of their long, sticky tongue.

SURVIVAL Most tree frogs are not endangered. However, as rain forests are cut down to make way for roads and agriculture, the habitat of tree frogs is lost. This may put these forest creatures at risk in the future.

Tadpoles develop inside a jelly-like mass of frog eggs on a leaf. After the tadpoles hatch, they mature into frogs.

FACTS AT A GLANCE

HABITAT Among the leaves in the canopy of the rain forest in tropical regions around the world

LIFESPAN 5 years in the wild

SIZE Average 3 inches (almost 8 centimeters)

DIET Crickets, flies, and other insects caught with a sticky tongue

Golden poison dart frogs range in color from bright yellow to pale green. Scientists are exploring ways to use the venom of these frogs to create a powerful painkiller.

ANIMAL BITES

THE **SKIN** OF A GOLDEN
POISON DART FROG
CONTAINS ENOUGH
TOXINS TO KILL
UP TO **20** PEOPLE.

EUROPE

Europe is 3,841,000 square miles (9,947,000 square kilometers) in area. It makes up almost 7 percent of Earth's land area. Only the continent of Australia is smaller. Europe is made up of many islands and peninsulas as well as broad plains and rugged mountains. These features provide the continent with diverse ecosystems. Among the many animals that call Europe home is this Eagle Owl, here soaring on silent wings at dusk.

ANIMAL BITES

EAGLE OWLS EAT
ALMOST **ANYTHING**
THEY CAN CATCH.
THEY HAVE BEEN KNOWN
TO EAT FOXES, DUCKS,
CRABS, SNAKES, AND
**EVEN OTHER
OWLS.**

Where Animals Live in
EUROPE

The great variety of physical environments in Europe contributes to many different ecosystems. From the cold north to the warm Mediterranean shores, thousands of creatures live in these environments.

TUNDRA The Arctic Fox lives in the cold tundra, where temperatures fall below -50°F (-46°C) in winter. The fox uses its bushy tail to stay warm.

DESERT The Saiga Antelope has a light brown summer coat, but a white winter coat. Its unusual bulging nose filters the dusty summer air and warms the freezing winter air.

MOUNTAIN In summer, herds of Chamois graze in high alpine meadows, but in winter they migrate to lower elevations.

FOREST The Nightingale is a morning songbird that is common in the forests of Europe. But in the winter months it migrates to Africa.

GRASSLAND The Iberian Lynx is a relative of the North American bobcat. It is the most endangered member of the cat family. The remaining Iberian lynxes are found on the Iberian Peninsula.

WETLAND Eurasian Otters spend much of the time in freshwater streams and lakes in forest areas. They live in dens called holts and eat fish. They hunt mainly at night.

Chamois

Arctic Fox

Saiga Antelope

Nightingale

Eurasian Otter

Iberian Lynx

Iceland

ATLANTIC OCEAN

Ireland

Great Britain

North Sea

Pyrenees

IBERIAN PENINSULA

Sardinia

M e d

Red dot indicates an animal at risk.

Eagle Owl / Chamois / Arctic Fox / Saiga Antelope / Nightingale / Eurasian Otter / Iberian Lynx

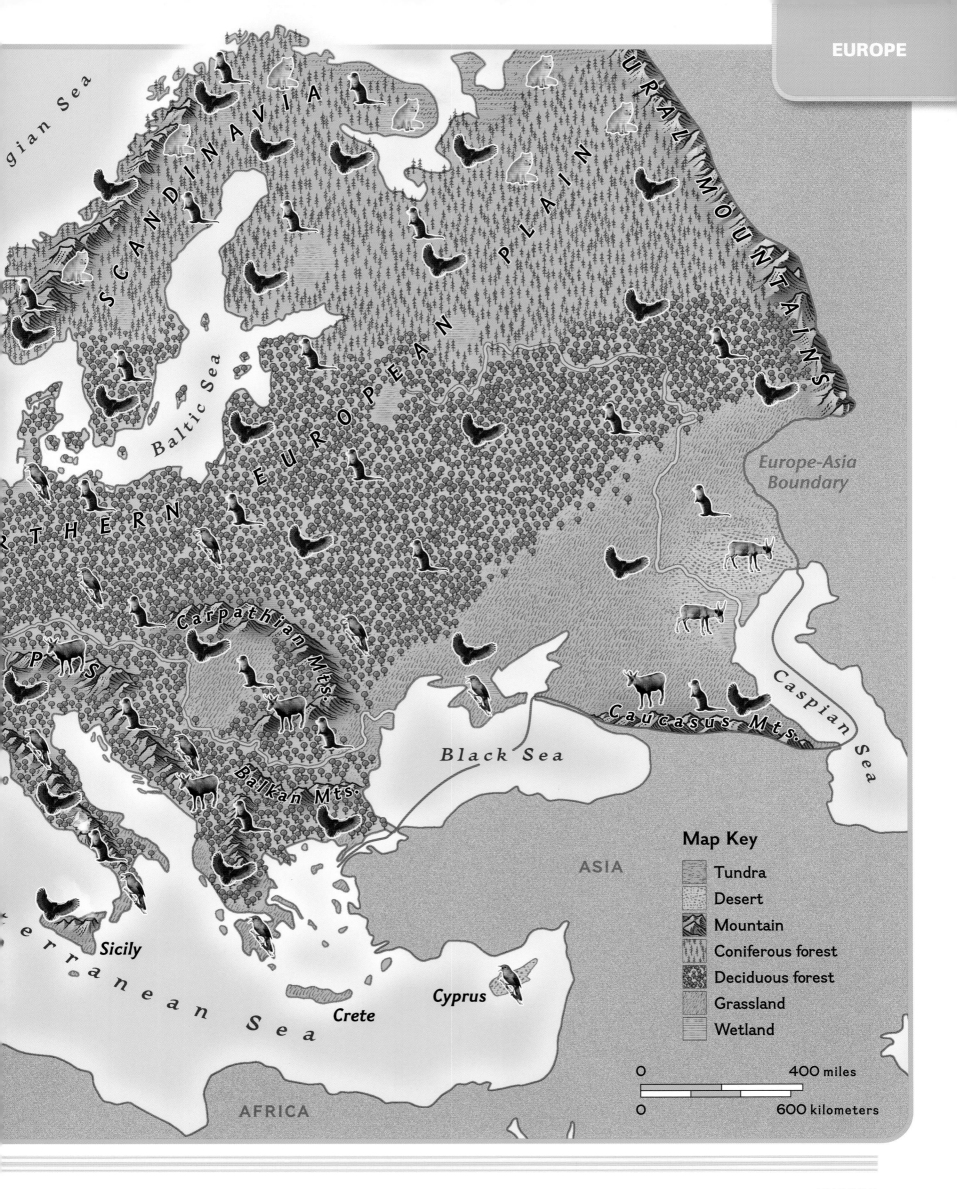

gian Sea

URAL MOUNTAINS

SCANDINAVIA

NORTHERN EUROPEAN PLAIN

Baltic Sea

Europe-Asia Boundary

Carpathian Mts.

P S

Caucasus Mts.

Caspian Sea

Balkan Mts.

Black Sea

ASIA

Sicily

terranean Sea

Crete

Cyprus

Map Key

Tundra

Desert

Mountain

Coniferous forest

Deciduous forest

Grassland

Wetland

0   400 miles

0   600 kilometers

AFRICA

THE ALPS

The Alps are mountains that stretch across south-central Europe from eastern France into eastern Europe. The rugged terrain creates many different ecosystems, ranging from snowy peaks to high meadows and low valleys.

EUROPE
Alps

AFRICA

| 0 | 400 miles |
| 0 | 400 kilometers |

Snow zone
(snow and ice)

9,800 feet (3,000 meters)

Alpine zone
(ibex)

6,500 feet (2,000 meters)

**Sub-alpine zone/
Arable zone**
(pine marten)

3,300 feet (1,000 meters)

Lowlands zone
(alpine marmot)

**ZONES OF THE
ALPS MOUNTAINS**

Animal at risk

ANIMAL BITES

THE ALPS HAVE
MORE THAN
30,000
ANIMAL SPECIES AND
13,000 PLANT SPECIES,
MAKING IT A BIODIVERSITY
HOTSPOT.

SALAMANDER
These amphibians look like a cross between a lizard and a frog. They live in cool, moist forests.

APOLLO BUTTERFLY
This butterfly lives in alpine meadows because it needs warmth from the sun in order to fly.

ALPINE MARMOT
Marmots live in family groups in alpine meadows and pastures. They spend much of the year in hibernation.

GOLDEN EAGLE

This large bird soars on updrafts in mountainous terrain. It uses sharp talons to catch small mammals.

ALPINE IBEX

The male ibex has long curved horns; the female's horns are short. Ibex live on rugged mountain slopes.

ROCK PTARMIGAN

This bird lives on rocky mountain slopes. Its feathers change from white in winter to brown in summer.

CAPERCAILLIE

These birds are clumsy fliers because of their short wings and heavy bodies. They eat mainly berries.

PINE MARTIN

This member of the weasel family is about the size of a cat. Its main food is mice.

ANIMAL BITES

OTTERS ARE VERY **PLAYFUL.** SOMETIMES THEY **PLAY "TAG,"** SLIDE DOWN **MUD** BANKS, OR SLIP AND SLIDE IN THE **SNOW.**

EURASIAN OTTERS

Otters, with their webbed feet, are excellent swimmers and spend a lot of time in water.

Otters are sometimes referred to as the clowns of the animal kingdom because of their playful antics on land and in the water. The Eurasian otter has short legs and a long body that is covered with thick brown fur. Each webbed paw has five toes that help make the otter an excellent swimmer. Otters typically have two to three cubs in a litter. The cubs stay with their mother until they are about one year old.

Eurasian Otter range

PACIFIC OCEAN

0   3,000 miles   INDIAN OCEAN

0   3,000 kilometers

HABITAT The Eurasian otter is the most widespread member of the otter family. Otters live in freshwater streams and ponds as well as in coastal areas. Otters dig burrows called holts in the banks of rivers. They are found throughout Europe, and also in Asia and North Africa.

Otters have thick fur that makes them well-adapted to cold winters. They even seem to enjoy playing in the snow.

DIET The Eurasian otter, like its cousins around the world, lives on a diet made up mainly of fish. But it also eats other aquatic life, as well as small birds, insects, and frogs. In fact, otters will eat almost anything they can hold. Their diet tends to vary, depending on what is readily available.

SURVIVAL Eurasian otters are at risk from humans, large birds of prey, such as eagles and falcons, and large meat-eating animals, such as lynxes and wolves. Humans also hunt them for their fur.

FACTS AT A GLANCE

HABITAT Freshwater streams and coastal areas throughout Europe, Asia, and North Africa

LIFESPAN Up to 22 years in captivity

SIZE 15 to 22 pounds (7 to 10 kilograms)

DIET Mainly fish, but also other aquatic life, including amphibians

These young otters appear curious about their environment. When otters are about ten weeks old, they venture out of the nest.

ASIA

sia is 17,208,000 square miles (44,570,000 square kilometers) in area. It is the largest of all the continents and makes up 30 percent of Earth's land area. Asia stretches all the way from the icy shores of the Arctic Ocean to the waters of the Indian and Pacific Oceans. Its many ecosystems range from mountains to tropical forests and deserts, with an equally broad range of animals living there, including the majestic but endangered Bengal Tiger.

Where Animals Live in

ASIA

Caribou

Asia's vast expanse includes many ecosystems, ranging from cold to hot, and wet to dry. Many different animals, birds, and fish live on the land, in the skies, or in the waters of this continent.

TUNDRA Caribou are members of the deer family. Unlike other deer, both males and females have antlers. Caribou migrate hundreds of miles in search of food and use their large hooves to dig through the snow for food during the long winters.

Bactrian Camel

DESERT Bactrian Camels live in the rocky deserts of Central Asia. They rely on fat stored in two humps on their back when water and food are not available.

Yak

MOUNTAIN Yaks live at elevations up to 19,000 feet (5,791 meters) in the mountains and plateaus of Tibet. Their broad hooves and heavy, woolly coat are adaptations to the extremes of the mountain environment.

Fishing Cat

FOREST Giant Pandas live in forests with a dense understory of bamboo, their favorite food. Pandas are endangered, with fewer than 2,000 remaining in the wild.

GRASSLAND Unlike its African relative, the **Greater One-horned Asian Rhinoceros** has just one horn. Its diet is mainly grasses, leaves, and fruits. This rhino is endangered, with only about 2,000 remaining in the wild.

Giant Panda

WETLAND The **Fishing Cat** lives near marshes and streams where it hunts birds, small mammals, snakes, and fish. It dives into the water and uses partially webbed paws to catch prey.

Greater One-horned Asian Rhinoceros

Mediterranean Sea

EUROPE

Black Sea

Europe-Asia Boundary

Caspian Sea

Red Sea

ARABIAN PENINSULA

Arabian Sea

INDIAN

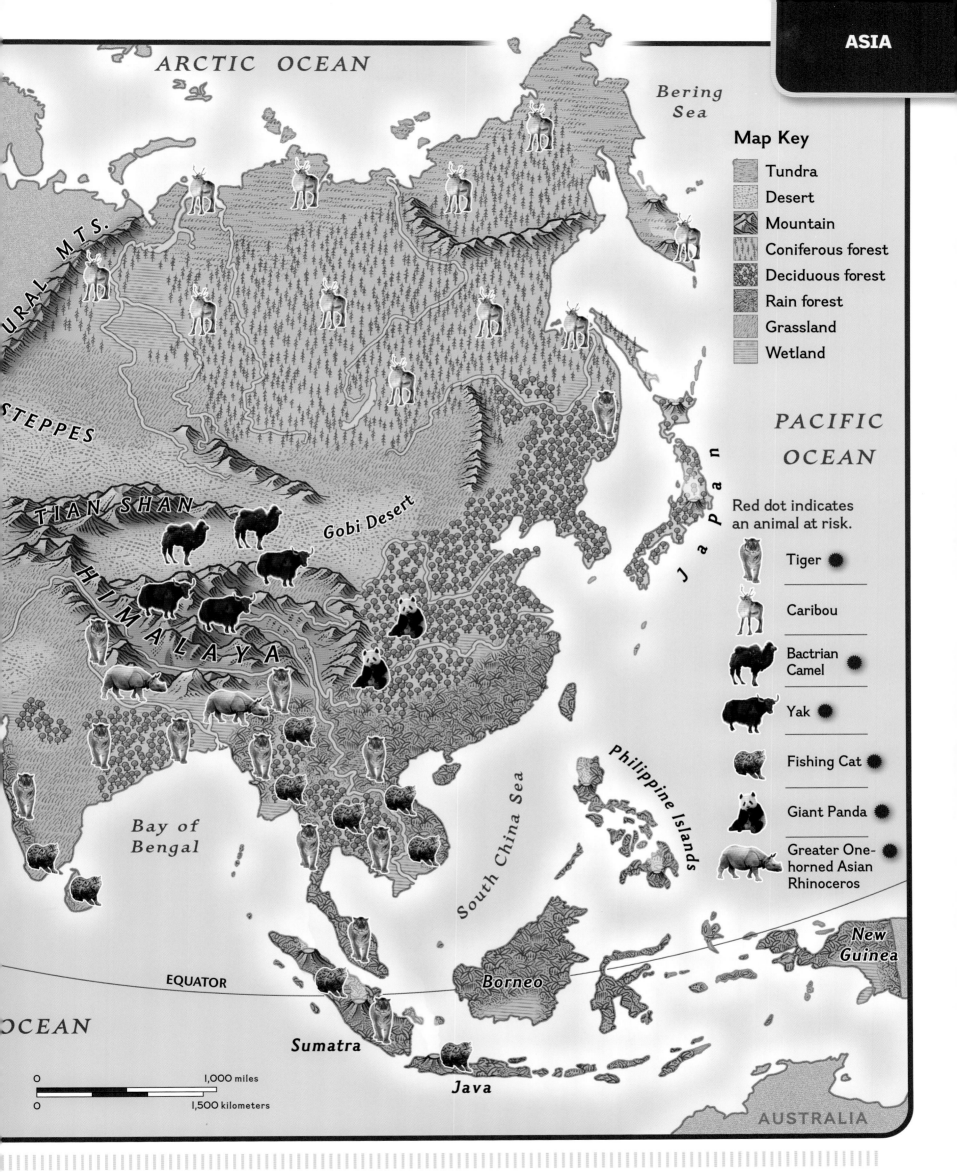

ARCTIC OCEAN

Bering
Sea

URAL MTS.

STEPPES

TIAN SHAN

HIMALAYA

Gobi Desert

Bay of
Bengal

South China Sea

Philippine Islands

Japan

PACIFIC

OCEAN

Borneo

New
Guinea

EQUATOR

Sumatra

Java

OCEAN

AUSTRALIA

Map Key

Tundra
Desert
Mountain
Coniferous forest
Deciduous forest
Rain forest
Grassland
Wetland

Red dot indicates
an animal at risk.

Tiger ●
Caribou
Bactrian
Camel ●
Yak ●
Fishing Cat ●
Giant Panda ●
Greater One-
horned Asian
Rhinoceros ●

0   1,000 miles
0   1,500 kilometers

THE GANGES DELTA

he Ganges Delta is made up of rich soil deposited by the Ganges and Brahmaputra Rivers. A vast wetland has formed where the rivers enter the Bay of Bengal. The seasonal rains of the summer monsoon often cause serious flooding in the delta.

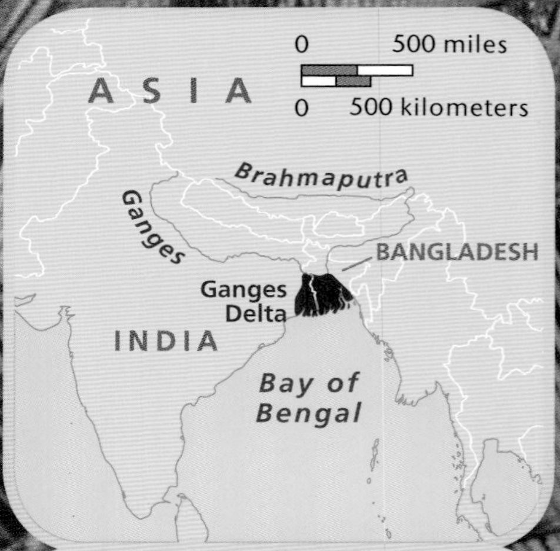

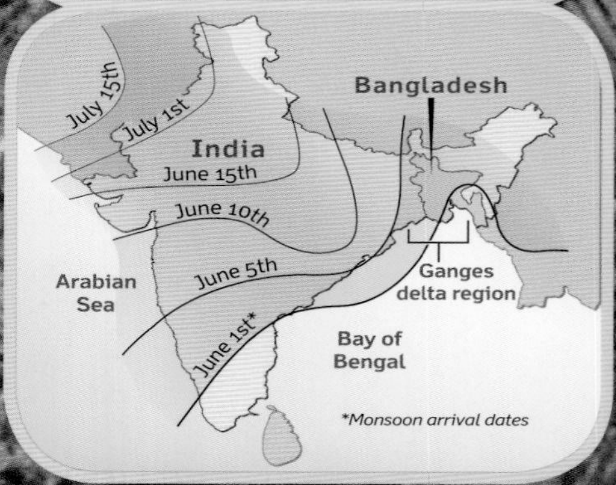

MONSOON ARRIVALS IN THE GANGES DELTA AND SOUTH ASIA

WILD BOAR
These wild pigs live in forested areas. They are a main food source for tigers and leopards.

CHITAL
This deer is common in forests of India. It has three-pronged antlers that are shed each year.

MUGGER CROCODILE
A clear, third eyelid allows these large crocodiles to keep their eyes open while swimming under water.

ANIMAL BITES

THE GANGES DELTA IS SHAPED LIKE A **TRIANGLE.** THE MIDDLE OF THE DELTA IS MADE UP OF SWAMPS, FORESTS, SMALL ISLANDS, AND CREEKS.

Animal at risk

BLACK-CROWNED NIGHT HERON
This bird has a black cap, yellow legs, and red eyes. It has a shorter bill than other herons.

BLUE-EARED KINGFISHER
This small bird, with bright blue feathers, catches fish in pools and streams in the tropical forests.

OLIVE RIDLEY TURTLE
This small sea turtle gets its name from the color of its heart-shaped shell, called a carapace.

GANGES RIVER DOLPHIN
This animal's eyes have no lenses, so it is blind. It is endangered because of pollution in the delta.

INDIAN PYTHON
This snake kills its prey by squeezing it. It may not eat again for a year.

GIANT PANDAS

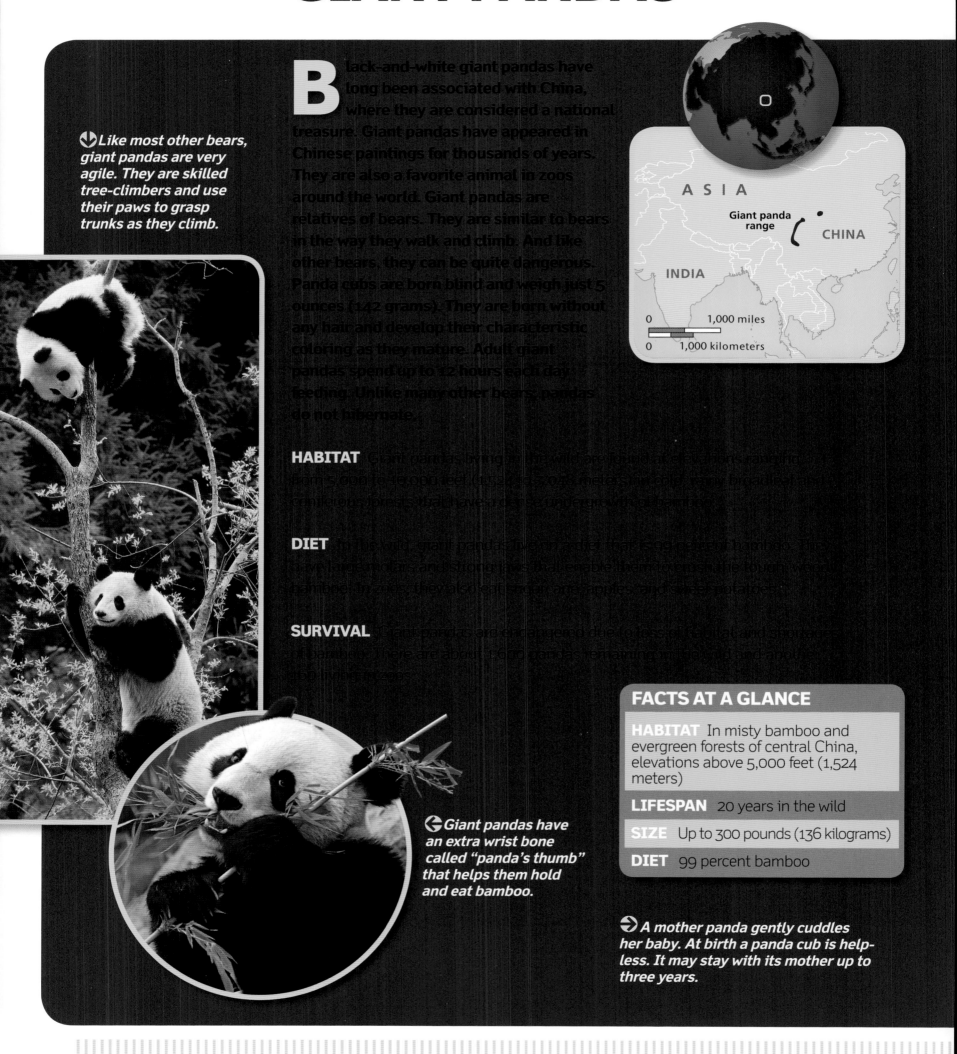

Like most other bears, giant pandas are very agile. They are skilled tree-climbers and use their paws to grasp trunks as they climb.

Black-and-white giant pandas have long been associated with China, where they are considered a national treasure. Giant pandas have appeared in Chinese paintings for thousands of years. They are also a favorite animal in zoos around the world. Giant pandas are relatives of bears. They are similar to bears in the way they walk and climb. And like other bears, they can be quite dangerous. Panda cubs are born blind and weigh just 5 ounces (142 grams). They are born without any hair and develop their characteristic coloring as they mature. Adult giant pandas spend up to 12 hours each day feeding. Unlike many other bears, pandas do not hibernate.

HABITAT Giant pandas living in the wild are found at elevations ranging from 5,000 to 10,000 feet (1,524 to 3,048 meters) but only many broadleaf and coniferous forests that have a dense undergrowth of bamboo.

DIET In the wild, giant pandas live on a diet that is comprised of bamboo. The strong jaws and strong teeth that enable them to crush the tough woody bamboo. In zoos, they also eat cereal grains, apples, and sweet potatoes.

SURVIVAL Giant pandas are endangered due to loss of habitat and shortage of bamboo. There are about 1,600 pandas remaining in the wild and around 300 living in zoos.

ASIA

Giant panda range

CHINA

INDIA

0   1,000 miles

0   1,000 kilometers

Giant pandas have an extra wrist bone called "panda's thumb" that helps them hold and eat bamboo.

FACTS AT A GLANCE

HABITAT In misty bamboo and evergreen forests of central China, elevations above 5,000 feet (1,524 meters)

LIFESPAN 20 years in the wild

SIZE Up to 300 pounds (136 kilograms)

DIET 99 percent bamboo

A mother panda gently cuddles her baby. At birth a panda cub is helpless. It may stay with its mother up to three years.

ANIMAL BITES

PANDAS MAKE A
BLEATING
SOUND SIMILAR TO A
LAMB OR A GOAT KID.
IT'S A **FRIENDLY**
NOISE THEY USE
TO GREET EACH OTHER.

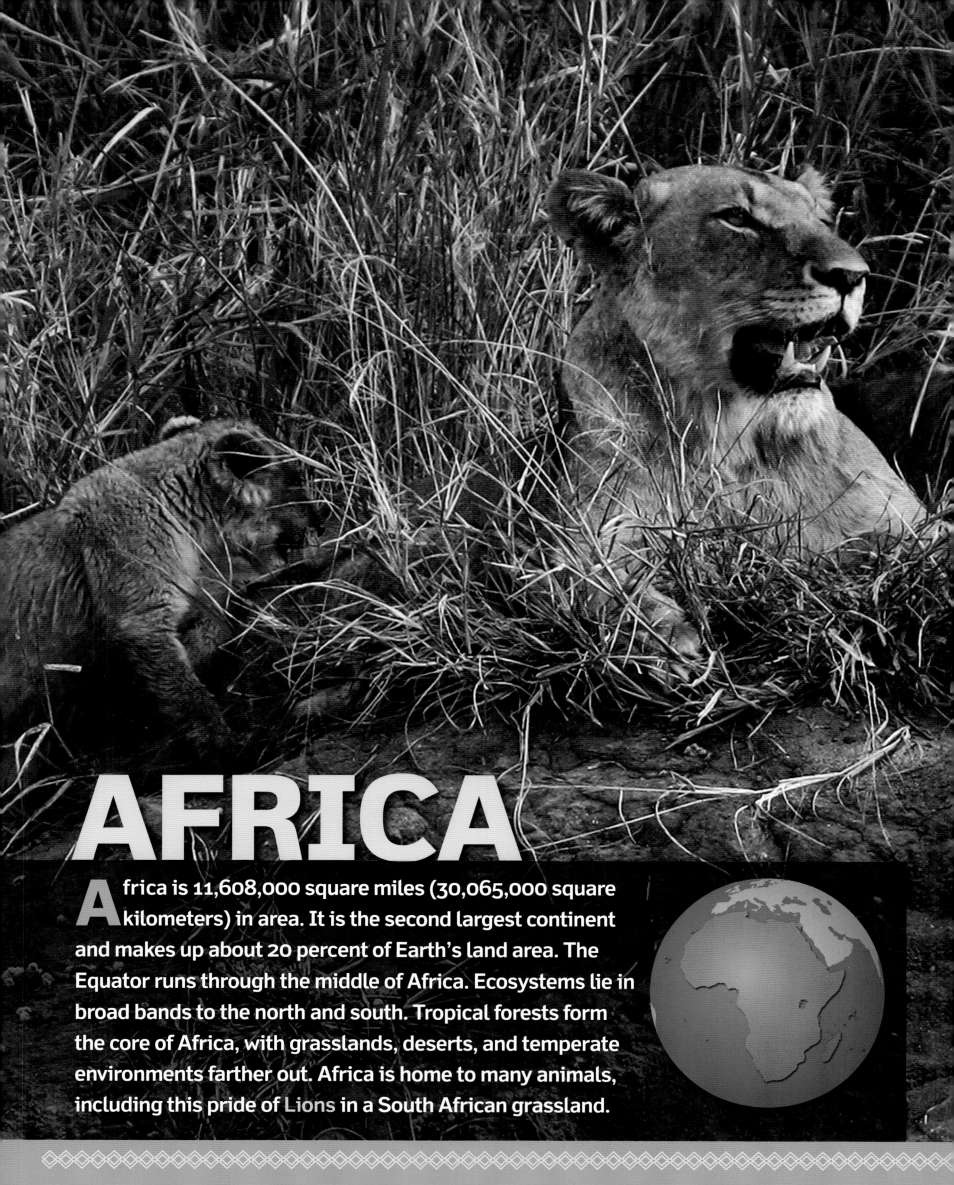

AFRICA

Africa is 11,608,000 square miles (30,065,000 square kilometers) in area. It is the second largest continent and makes up about 20 percent of Earth's land area. The Equator runs through the middle of Africa. Ecosystems lie in broad bands to the north and south. Tropical forests form the core of Africa, with grasslands, deserts, and temperate environments farther out. Africa is home to many animals, including this pride of Lions in a South African grassland.

ANIMAL BITES

A MOTHER LION TAKES CARE OF HER **MALE** CUBS FOR ABOUT **TWO YEARS,** BUT **FEMALE** CUBS MAY LIVE WITH THEIR MOTHER FOR **LIFE.**

AFRICA

Africa includes many different ecosystems, but it has no extremely cold environments. The continent is a rich blend of mammals, birds, and fish living in different environments on the land, in the air, or in the water.

DESERT The Spiny-Tailed Lizard is a desert dweller. It tolerates hot days and chilly nights. It eats leaves, seeds, and insects, but requires very little water. Some varieties reach 30 inches (76 centimeters) in length.

MOUNTAIN Gorillas live near the Equator on mountain slopes and in bamboo forests, as well as in lowland rain forests. They live in groups called troops, led by a large male called a "silverback."

FOREST Chimpanzees live in social communities of several dozen animals in the rain forests and woodlands of central and western Africa. Among all creatures of the animal kingdom, they are the most closely related to humans.

GRASSLAND Many animals associated with Africa, such as Zebras and Cheetahs, are found in tropical grasslands called savannas. Zebras are grass-eaters. But cheetahs are meat eaters that hunt other grassland animals for their food.

WETLAND The Hippopotamus lives in rivers and lakes of Africa. On land it can outrun the fastest human, at least for a short distance. Hippos spend their days in the water, but come out at night to graze on land.

Cheetah

Gorilla

Zebra

Hippopotamus

Spiny-Tailed Lizard

Chimpanzee

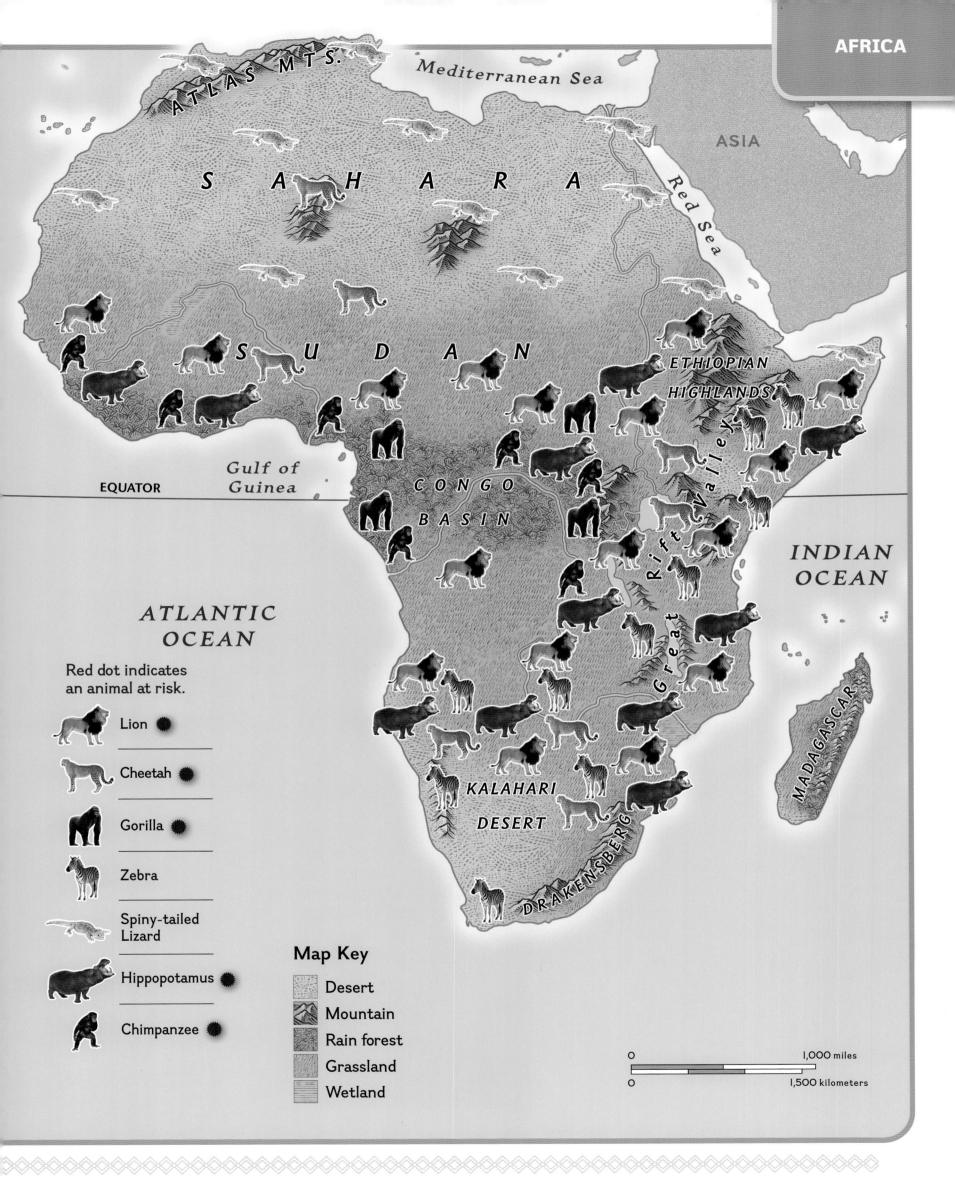

ATLAS MTS.

Mediterranean Sea

ASIA

S A H A R A

Red Sea

S U D A N

ETHIOPIAN
HIGHLANDS

EQUATOR

Gulf of
Guinea

CONGO

BASIN

Rift Valley

INDIAN
OCEAN

ATLANTIC
OCEAN

Great

MADAGASCAR

Red dot indicates
an animal at risk.

Lion ●

Cheetah ●

Gorilla ●

Zebra

Spiny-tailed
Lizard

Hippopotamus ●

Chimpanzee ●

KALAHARI

DESERT

DRAKENSBERG

Map Key

Desert

Mountain

Rain forest

Grassland

Wetland

0   1,000 miles

0   1,500 kilometers

THE SAVANNA

The African savanna is home to many of Earth's big game animals. It is a grassland with two seasons—wet and dry. Towering above the savanna in Tanzania is Kilimanjaro, Africa's highest mountain.

AFRICA

Savanna

EQUATOR

ATLANTIC OCEAN

Savanna

0   1,000 miles

0   1,000 kilometers

grasses

scavenger (hyena)

grass eater (zebra)

meat eater (lion)

FOOD WEB OF THE AFRICAN SAVANNA

HORNBILL
Named for their large curved bills, hornbills live on a diet of fruit, insects, and small animals.

GIRAFFE
With its long legs and neck, the giraffe is Earth's tallest animal. It grazes on tree leaves instead of grasses.

GABOON VIPER
This poisonous member of the puff adder family has the longest fangs of any snake on Earth.

HYENA
This scavenger animal is a skilled hunter but often eats scraps left by other hunters of the savanna.

Animal at risk

ANIMAL BITES

THE ACACIA TREE SURVIVES
DROUGHT BECAUSE ITS
LONG ROOTS
REACH WATER SOURCES
DEEP
UNDERGROUND.

IMPALA
Male impalas use their long horns to fight other males for territory and control of the herd.

AFRICAN ELEPHANT
The largest land animals on Earth, African elephants use their trunks to spray water to keep cool.

SAVANNA HARE
Keen hearing and smell help the savanna hare avoid predators. Hares eat leaves, roots, berries, and bark.

WILDEBEEST
Also known as a gnu, this member of the antelope family grazes in large herds on the savanna.

ANIMAL BITES

CHIMPS MAKE
A GRUNTING SOUND
WHEN THEY ARE
HAPPY.
A TOOTHY "GRIN"
ACTUALLY INDICATES
FEAR OR
ANXIETY.

CHIMPANZEES

Chimpanzees are very intelligent animals. They often behave in ways that remind us of humans. Chimpanzees are one of the few animals that use tools. They often use sticks to dig insects out of the ground. They also use stones to crack open nuts. Some chimpanzees have even learned to communicate with humans using simple sign language. Because they can be taught to perform many different tasks, chimpanzees are often used in scientific studies. In fact, the first "American" in space was actually a chimpanzee named Ham who orbited Earth in 1961.

◐ *A chimpanzee in Africa clings to a tree as it watches something on the ground below. A chimp's facial expression often shows human-like emotion.*

AFRICA

Chimpanzee range

ATLANTIC
OCEAN

0   1,000 miles

0   1,000 kilometers

HABITAT Chimpanzees live in many different forest settings in western and central Africa. They live in steamy tropical rain forests. But they also thrive in lowland and mountain forests. Chimpanzees live in family groups of 6 to 10 individuals. These family groups live in communities that may include as many as 100 members.

▽ *A female chimpanzee cradles her three-month-old baby. Young chimps stay with their mothers until they are seven years old.*

DIET Chimpanzees enjoy a varied diet. They mainly eat fruit, seeds, leaves, bark, and insects. But they also eat meat and eggs. Chimpanzees usually search for food alone, but sometimes they hunt in small groups.

SURVIVAL Chimpanzees are considered an endangered species. Expanding human populations have destroyed their natural habitat. People also hunt chimpanzees for food.

FACTS AT A GLANCE

HABITAT Tropical rain forests, as well as lowland and mountain forests of western and central Africa

LIFESPAN An average of 45 years in the wild, but up to 50 years in zoos

SIZE 4 to 5.5 feet (about 1 to 2 meters) tall

DIET Fruits, plants, insects, eggs, meat

➡ *Strong arms and hands that can grip allow these chimpanzees in a park in Nigeria to swing from vines and tree branches.*

AUSTRALIA

Australia is 2,970,000 square miles (7,692,000 square kilometers) in area. It is the smallest of all the continents and makes up just over 5 percent of Earth's land area. Australia's closest neighbors are New Zealand and other island countries of the South Pacific Ocean region. Because of its relatively remote location, Australia has many unusual animals, such as these furry Koalas that are found in the wild nowhere else on Earth.

ANIMAL BITES

WHEN A KOALA IS
BORN IT IS ABOUT
THE SIZE OF
A BIG **JELLY BEAN.**
IT CAN'T SEE OR HEAR,
BUT IT CAN
CLIMB!

AUSTRALIA

Dingo

Australia's interior is desert and dry grasslands. Coastal areas receive ample rainfall and have more vegetation. The continent has many unique mammals, birds, and fish that live in different environments.

DESERT Galah Cockatoos live in the desert and semi-arid interior of Australia. This colorful bird generally feeds on the ground, eating seeds of melons and pines that are found near water sources. Dingoes are wild dogs that have lived in Australia for at least 15,000 years. Although they howl, dingoes do not bark like other dogs. They eat small animals, which they hunt mainly at night.

Galah Cockatoo

MOUNTAIN Wombats live in burrows in mountainous forested areas of south-eastern Australia. Babies live in a pouch on the mother's belly for five months. Wombats come out at night to feed on grasses, roots, and bark.

Wombat

FOREST The Brushtail Possum is a nocturnal animal, meaning it sleeps during the day and is active at night. It lives high in the trees on a diet of leaves, fruit, buds, and bark.

Kangaroo

GRASSLAND Kangaroos use their powerful hind legs to hop through the grasslands and desert margins of Australia. Male red kangaroos can be more than 5 feet (1.5 meters) tall. A group of kangaroos is called a mob.

Brushtail Possum

Platypus

WETLAND Platypuses are very unusual animals. They have a bill and webbed feet like a duck and a tail like a beaver. They live in land burrows, but they are good swimmers and hunt food under water.

INDIAN OCEAN

Great De

W

P

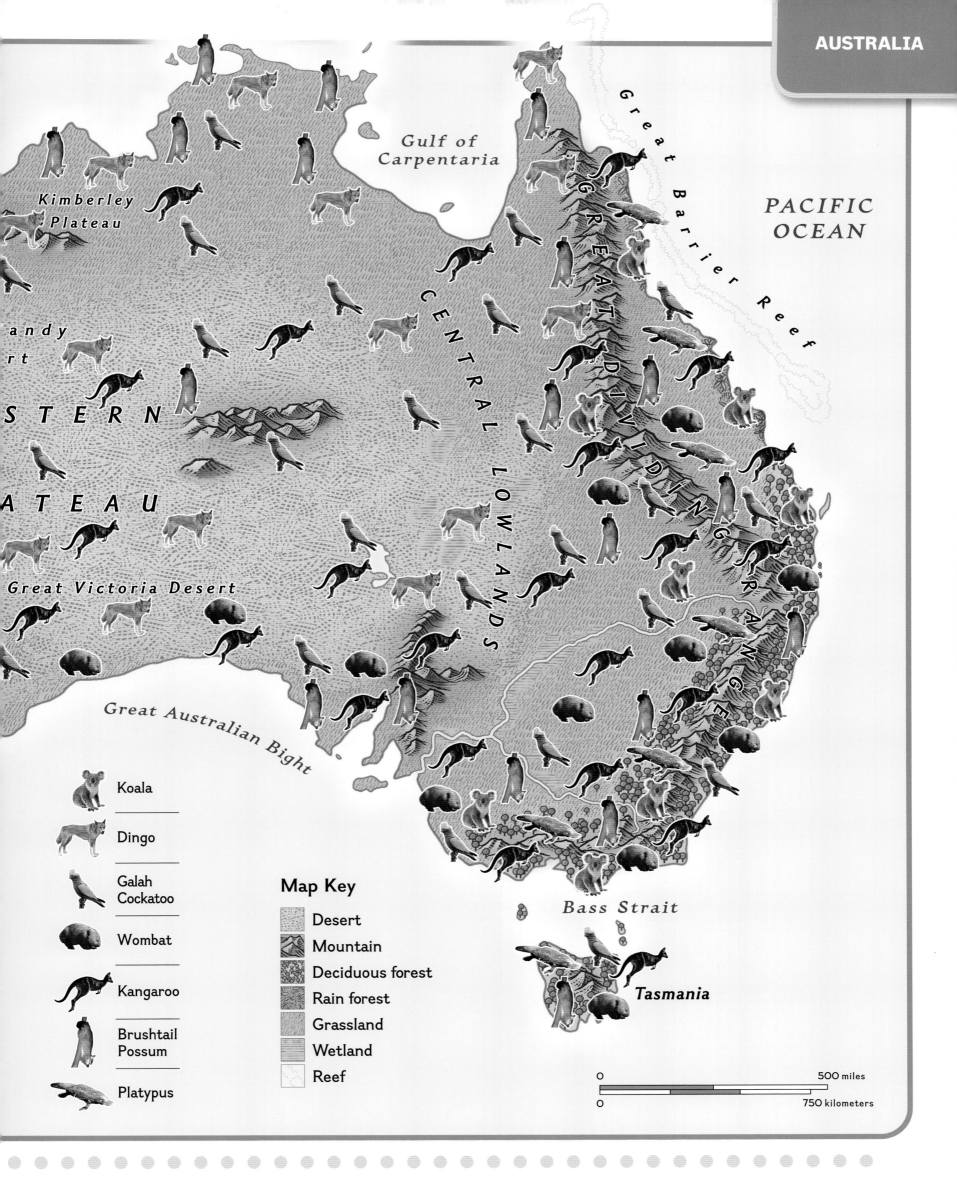

Gulf of
Carpentaria

PACIFIC
OCEAN

Great Barrier Reef

*Kimberley
Plateau*

G R E A T

*andy
rt*

STERN

ATEAU

CENTRAL LOWLANDS

D I V I D I N G

Great Victoria Desert

R A N G E

Great Australian Bight

Bass Strait

Tasmania

Koala

Dingo

Galah
Cockatoo

Wombat

Kangaroo

Brushtail
Possum

Platypus

Map Key

Desert

Mountain

Deciduous forest

Rain forest

Grassland

Wetland

Reef

0   500 miles

0   750 kilometers

THE GREAT BARRIER REEF

Stretching more than 1,400 miles (2,200 kilometers) along Australia's northeast coast, the Great Barrier Reef is made of skeletons of tiny marine animals called corals. The reef is home to many different sea animals.

Great Barrier Reef

AUSTRALIA

0   500 miles

0   500 kilometers

reef face   reef crest   patch reef   lagoon

ZONES OF THE GREAT BARRIER REEF

● Animal at risk

ANIMAL BITES

CORAL REEFS ARE CONSIDERED THE **RAIN FORESTS** OF THE SEA BECAUSE THEY PROVIDE FOOD AND SHELTER FOR UP TO **25 PERCENT** OF ALL MARINE LIFE.

LEATHERBACK SEA TURTLE
Leatherbacks can dive to depths of 4,200 feet (1,280 meters) and stay down as long as 85 minutes.

BOX JELLYFISH
Stinging cells on each tentacle of this jellyfish deliver one of the most deadly toxins on Earth.

BLACK-TIPPED REEF SHARK
These sharks swim in shallow water, hunting for fish among the coral reefs. They try to avoid swimmers.

WHITE-BELLIED SEA EAGLE
These large birds mate for life. They use their sharp talons to snatch fish from the water.

BOTTLENOSE DOLPHIN
These dolphins swim up to 18 miles (29 kilometers) an hour. They must surface often to breathe.

ANEMONEFISH
Known as a clownfish because of its colorful markings, this fish lives among the tentacles of the sea anemone.

DUGONG
These large aquatic mammals can stay underwater up to 8 minutes while they graze on sea grasses.

BROWN STINGRAY
This relative of sharks uses the sharp barb on the end of its tail to defend itself.

KANGAROOS

Kangaroos are the only large animals on Earth that travel by hopping across the landscape. Red kangaroos, the largest of all kangaroos, are known to cover up to 25 feet (almost 8 meters) and jump up to 6 feet (almost 2 meters) high in a single leap. Throughout Australia, there are many different types of kangaroos, including the wallaby, a smaller relative. Kangaroos, along with koalas and wombats, belong to the marsupial family of animals. This means that after their young are born, they live in a pouch on the mother's belly until they are old enough to live on their own. At birth, a baby kangaroo is only about the size of a cherry.

While balancing on their tails, male kangaroos use their short front legs and strong hind legs to "box" with other males.

Kangaroo range

AUSTRALIA

0   1,000 miles

0   1,000 kilometers

HABITAT Kangaroos live in many different environments throughout Australia. They can be found in forests and grasslands, as well as in the desert of interior Australia and the tropical forests of northern Australia. Kangaroos live in groups, called mobs, of only a few members or as many as 100 animals.

DIET Kangaroos are herbivores, meaning they eat only plant material. Much like cattle and sheep, they graze mainly on grasses, but also eat leaves, shrubs, and twigs. They have specially adapted teeth for chewing grasses and stems.

SURVIVAL
Kangaroos are found throughout Australia, but they are increasingly at risk due to loss of habitat as humans develop more and more land. In addition, kangaroo meat is becoming a popular human food.

FACTS AT A GLANCE

HABITAT Only in Australia in the wild; adapted to various environments, including forests, grasslands, and deserts

LIFESPAN Up to 23 years in the wild

SIZE 3 to 5 feet (1 to almost 2 meters) tall

DIET Grasses, leaves, shrubs, twigs

Kangaroos use their powerful hind legs to hop across the landscape at more than 30 miles (48 kilometers) an hour.

A young kangaroo, called a joey, peeks from its mother's pouch. Babies spend up to 9 months in the pouch, living on the mother's milk.

ANIMAL BITES

KANGAROOS HAVE PLENTY OF **NICKNAMES.** A **FEMALE** IS CALLED A DOE, FLYER, JILL, OR ROO. A **MALE** KANGAROO IS CALLED A BUCK, BOOMER, JACK, OR OLD MAN.

ANIMAL BITES

EMPEROR PENGUINS
CAN'T FLY,
BUT THEY SURE CAN SWIM.
THESE PENGUINS
DIVE DEEPER THAN
ANY OTHER BIRD—UP TO
1,850 FEET
(565 METERS).

ANTARCTICA

Antarctica is 5,100,000 square miles (13,209,000 square kilometers) in area. It ranks fifth among all the continents and makes up almost 9 percent of Earth's land area. About 98 percent of Antarctica is buried beneath vast ice sheets that are nearly 3 miles (5 kilometers) thick in places. Despite forbidding cold and darkness for part of the year, Antarctica has many animals, including these Emperor Penguins that live on the coastal ice and water of Antarctica.

ANTARCTICA

Snow Petrel

Blue Whale

South Polar Skua

Leopard Seal

Humpback Whale

Although most of Antarctica lies under thick ice sheets and about half of the year is spent in darkness, the coastal ice and waters surrounding the continent are home to a wide variety of animal life.

KRILL Although they average only 2 inches (5 centimeters) long, these tiny sea creatures are a very important part of the global food chain, providing food for fish, birds, and whales.

LEOPARD SEAL These seals are named for their spots, which resemble those of a leopard. They are fierce predators that use their powerful jaws to capture smaller seals, fish, and squid.

WHALES These ocean giants are Earth's largest animals. They live on a diet of krill, consuming up to 4 tons daily. Blue Whales are the largest of all whales and live 80 to 90 years. Humpback Whales are known for their songs, which can be heard for great distances through the world's oceans.

EMPEROR PENGUIN The largest of all penguins, these flightless birds, the only animals that spend winters in Antarctica, huddle together to avoid the frigid temperatures of the continent.

SOUTH POLAR SKUA This bird, known for its powerful flight, is a fierce defender of its nesting territory. It feeds mainly on krill, small fish, and penguin eggs and chicks.

SNOW PETREL These birds are named for their snow-white feathers. They feed by skimming the surface of the cold ocean waters.

Krill

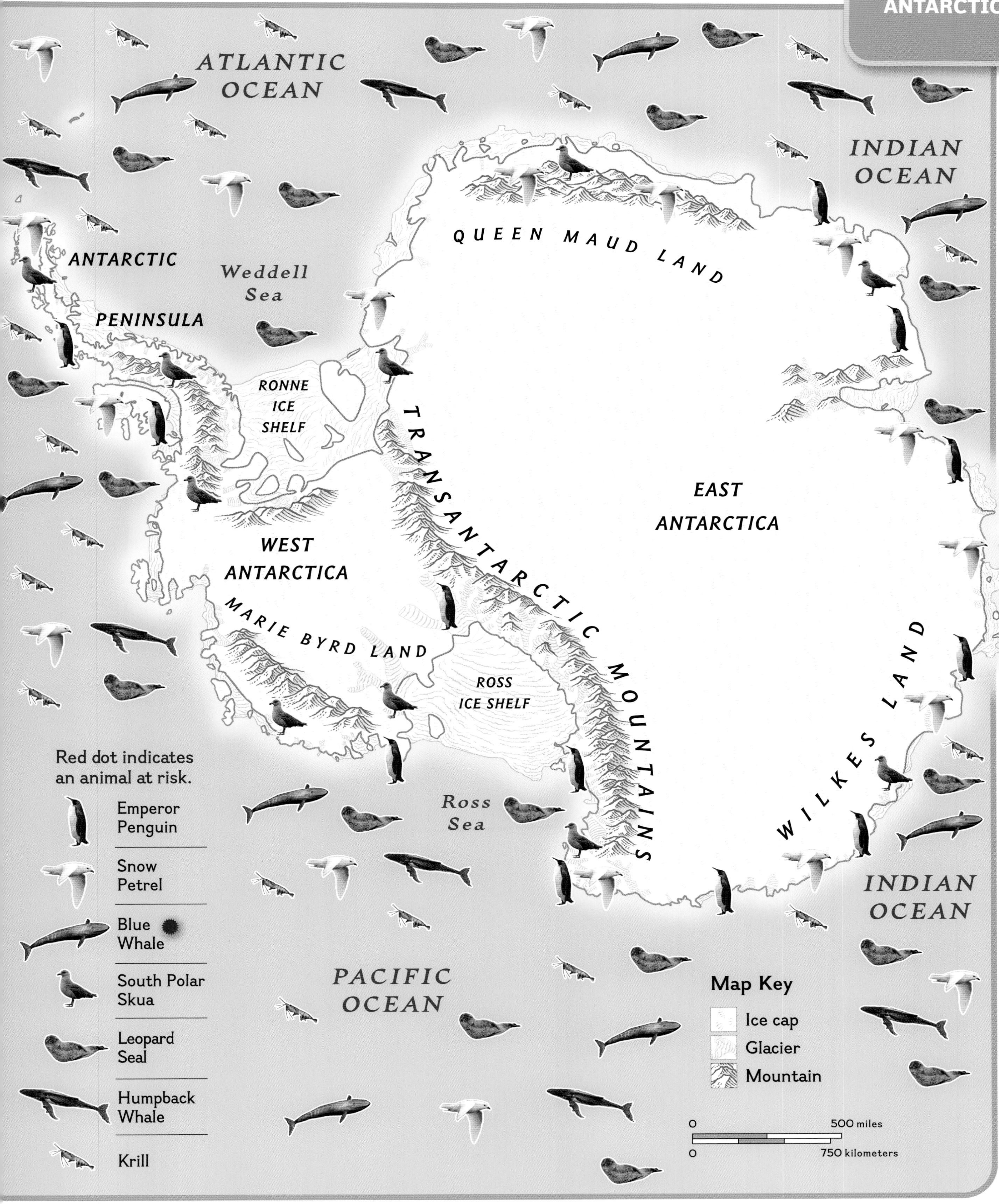

ATLANTIC
OCEAN

INDIAN
OCEAN

QUEEN MAUD LAND

ANTARCTIC

Weddell
Sea

PENINSULA

RONNE
ICE
SHELF

EAST
ANTARCTICA

T R A N S A N T A R C T I C   M O U N T A I N S

WEST
ANTARCTICA

W
I
L
K
E
S

L
A
N
D

MARIE BYRD LAND

ROSS
ICE SHELF

Ross
Sea

INDIAN
OCEAN

Red dot indicates
an animal at risk.

Emperor
Penguin

Snow
Petrel

Blue
Whale

South Polar
Skua

Leopard
Seal

Humpback
Whale

Krill

PACIFIC
OCEAN

Map Key

	Ice cap
	Glacier
	Mountain

0	500 miles
0	750 kilometers

ANIMAL BITES

WHEN A BLUE WHALE
EXHALES THROUGH
ITS BLOWHOLE, THE
WATER SPRAY
CAN REACH **30** FEET (9 METERS)
INTO THE AIR.

BLUE WHALES

The blue whale is the largest animal that has ever lived on Earth. These giants of the deep live in every ocean, moving through the water at more than 5 miles (8 kilometers) an hour. Their seasonal migrations can take them thousands of miles.

◉A blue whale, seen from above, can remain underwater for up to 20 minutes.

HABITAT Blue whales are found in all of Earth's oceans, including the waters around Antarctica, sometimes referred to as the Southern Ocean. They spend summers feeding in cold waters at high latitudes and migrate in winter toward low latitudes, where they breed.

The Blue whale range covers almost all oceans

ARCTIC OCEAN
ATLANTIC OCEAN
PACIFIC OCEAN
EQUATOR
PACIFIC OCEAN
INDIAN OCEAN
ANTARCTICA

◉Huge triangular tail fins, called flukes, rise in the air as this blue whale dives.

DIET Blue whales live almost entirely on tiny creatures called krill. An adult may eat as many as 40 million krill in a single day. Whales catch their food by diving into a school of krill with their mouths wide open. Then they squeeze out the water and swallow the krill, along with any fish or crustaceans that were also caught.

SURVIVAL Blue whales were once threatened by the whaling industry. Since the 1960s, hunting blue whales has been banned, but they are still considered endangered. Changing ocean temperatures associated with global warming may pose a new risk by reducing the supply of krill.

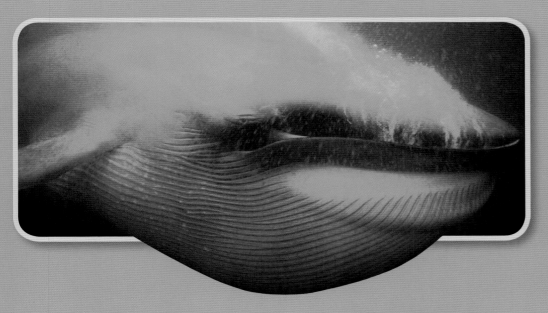

◉Pleated skin on a blue whale's throat and belly expands to take in huge amounts of water and krill while feeding.

FACTS AT A GLANCE

HABITAT Earth's oceans; feeding in polar regions in summer; migrating to the Equator as winter approaches.

LIFESPAN An average of 80 to 90 years in the wild

SIZE 82 to 105 feet (25 to 32 meters) long

DIET Shrimplike creatures called krill

Glossary

Adapted/adaptation: changing to fit an environment

Animal at risk: animals that are in danger of no longer being found in the wild because of loss of habitat or danger from humans

Canopy: the layer of a rain forest under the emergent layer. Trees in this layer of the rain forest grow from 65 to 130 feet (20 to 40 m) tall.

Carnivore: a meat-eating animal

Climate: average weather conditions of a region

Coniferous forest: evergreen, needleleaf trees that bear seeds in cones

Contiguous: touching along an unbroken boundary

Continent: one of the seven large pieces of land on Earth. These include North America, South America, Europe, Asia, Africa, Australia, and Antarctica

Coral reef: an underwater formation made of skeletons of coral and other natural substances

Deciduous forest: trees, such as oak and maple, that lose their leaves in the cold season

Deforestation: the process of cutting down forests

Delta: a triangle-shaped piece of land made of mud and sand at the mouth of a river

Ecosystem: a system of living things that live together and interact with their environment

Emergent layer: the tallest layer of a rain forest that grows above the canopy. Trees in this layer of the rain forest grow up to 270 feet (82 m) tall.

Environment: the air, water, plants, and animals that make up the natural life in an area

Extinction: the loss of one or more forms of life

Food web: the group of food chains that interact in an ecosystem

Forest floor: the bottom layer of a rain forest where fallen leaves, branches, stems and other natural materials are found

Global warming: warming of the Earth's air and water due in part to air pollution

Grassland: land covered in grasses instead of shrubs and trees

Growing season: the part of the year when it is warm enough for plants to grow

Habitat: a plant or animal's natural home

Herbivore: a plant-eating animal

High latitude: the part of Earth's surface that is closer to the North or South Pole

Ice cap: a thick layer of ice on land that flows out from its center

Island: land that is completely surrounded by water

Low latitude: the part of Earth's surface that is closer to the Equator

Majestic: extremely beautiful

Mammal: a warm-blooded animal that has hair and produces milk to feed its young

Mangrove: trees or shrubs in tropical areas that grow shallow salt water

Monsoon: winds that change direction seasonally, bringing heavy rain in summer

Omnivore: an animal that eats both plants and meat

Peninsula: land that sticks out into a body of water and is almost completely surrounded by water

Plateau: a broad, elevated area of flat land

Pollinate: to move pollen from one plant or flower to another

Predator: an animal that hunts and kills another animal for food

Prey: an animal that is hunted and killed by another animal for food

Pride: a group of lions

Rain forest: an area of forest with tall trees near the Equator that receives heavy rainfall

Reptile: a cold-blooded animal that has skin covered with scales or bony plates

Scavenger: an animal that feeds on the remains of dead animals

Shrub layer: layer of the rain forest below the understory with low-growing plants

Species: a group of plants or animals that share common characteristics

Temperate: an area of mild climate that does not have extremely hot or extremely cold weather

Temperature: the degree of hotness or coldness of an environment

Tundra: a region at high latitude or high elevation that has cold temperatures and low vegetation

Understory: trees and shrubs found between a forest canopy and the ground

Vegetation: the plants that live in a particular environment

Vulnerable: animals that are at risk of becoming endangered

Wetland: land that is either covered or soaked by water, such as swamps, for at least part of the year

Woodland: land covered with trees and shrubs

Resources

BOOKS

Earle, Sylvia. *Coral Reefs*. Washington, D.C.: National Geographic Children's Books, 2009.

First Discovery: Endangered Animals. New York: Scholastic, 2007.

Lauber, Patricia. *Who Eats What? Food Chains and Food Webs*. New York: HarperCollins Children's, 1994.

National Geographic Beginner's United States Atlas. Washington, D.C.: National Geographic Children's Books, 2009.

National Geographic Beginner's World Atlas. Washington, D.C.: National Geographic Children's Books, 2005.

National Geographic Kids Almanac 2010. Washington, D.C.: National Geographic Children's Books, 2009.

VanCleave, Janice. *Science Around the World: Activities on Biomes form Pole to Pole*. Hoboken, New Jersey: Wiley, 2004.

WEBSITES

Animal Corner
http://www.animalcorner.co.uk/index.html

Defenders of Wildlife
http://www.kidsplanet.org/

National Geographic
http://animals.nationalgeographic.com/animals/

National Geographic Atlas Web Site
http://www.nationalgeographic.com/kids-world-atlas/

National Geographic Kids
http://kids.nationalgeographic.com/Animals/

The National Zoo
http://nationalzoo.si.edu/Audiences/kids/

San Diego Zoo
http://www.sandiegozoo.org/kids/index.html

World Wildlife Fund
http://www.panda.org/about_our_earth/

Yahoo Kids
http://kids.yahoo.com/animals

Index

Published by the National Geographic Society

John M. Fahey, Jr.,
President and Chief Executive Officer

Gilbert M. Grosvenor, *Chairman of the Board*

Tim T. Kelly, *President, Global Media Group*

John Q. Griffin, *Executive Vice President; President, Publishing*

Nina D. Hoffman,
Executive Vice President; President, Book Publishing Group

Melina Gerosa Bellows,
Executive Vice President, Children's Publishing

Prepared by the Book Division

Nancy Laties Feresten,
Vice President, Editor in Chief, Children's Books

Jonathan Halling,
Design Director, Children's Publishing

Jennifer Emmett,
Executive Editor, Reference and Solo, Children's Books

Carl Mehler, *Director of Maps*

R. Gary Colbert, *Production Director*

Jennifer A. Thornton, *Managing Editor*

Staff for This Book

Priyanka Lamichhane, *Project Editor*
Lori Epstein, *Illustrations Editor*
David M. Seager, *Art Director*
Sven M. Dolling, Michael McNey, *XNR Productions, Map Research and Production*
Martha B. Sharma, *Writer and Consultant*
Stuart Armstrong, *Graphics Illustrator*
Grace Hill, *Associate Managing Editor*
Lewis R. Bassford, *Production Manager*
Kate Olesin, *Editorial Assistant*
Susan Borke, *Legal and Business Affairs*

Manufacturing and Quality Management

Christopher A. Liedel, *Chief Financial Officer*
Phillip L. Schlosser, *Vice President*
Chris Brown, *Technical Director*
Nicole Elliott, *Manager*
Rachel Faulise, *Manager*

Founded in 1888, the National Geographic Society is one of the largest nonprofit scientific and educational organizations in the world. It reaches more than 285 million people worldwide each month through its official journal, *National Geographic,* and its four other magazines; the National Geographic Channel; television documentaries; radio programs; films; books; videos and DVDs; maps; and interactive media. National Geographic has funded more than 8,000 scientific research projects and supports an education program combating geographic illiteracy.

For more information, please call 1-800-NGS LINE (647-5463) or write to the following address:

NATIONAL GEOGRAPHIC SOCIETY
1145 17th Street N.W., Washington, D.C. 20036-4688 U.S.A.

Visit us online at www.nationalgeographic.com/books

For information about special discounts for bulk purchases, please contact National Geographic Books Special Sales: ngspecsales@ngs.org

For rights or permissions inquiries, please contact National Geographic Books Subsidiary Rights: ngbookrights@ngs.org

A Note from the Publisher

National Geographic would like to thank veterinarian Dr. Lucy Spelman for her generous assistance and thoughtful review of this book.

COVER
Front Cover, (frog) Tim Flach/ Stone / Getty Images; (orangutan), Tim Flach/ Getty Images; (elephant), Frans Lanting/ Minden Pictures; (penguins), Konrad Wothe/ Minden Pictures/ NationalGeographicStock.com; (tiger), Tiago Estima/ iStockphoto.com; Back Cover, (road runner) Jill Fromer/ iStockphoto.com; (butterfly) Jens Stolt/ Shutterstock; (gorilla) Eric Gevaert/ Shutterstock; (ibex) Gertjan Hooijer/ iStockphoto.com; (chimpanzee) Eric Isselée/ Shutterstock; (macaw) Stephen Dalton/ Minden Pictures; (jaguar) Philip Dowell/ Dorling Kindersley; (panda) Eric Isselée/ Shutterstock; (lizard) fivespots/ Shutterstock; (frog) Dr. Morley Read/ Shutterstock; Dust Jacket, (buffalo) Tom Grundy/ Shutterstock; (fish) istockphoto.com; (hare) Mike Wilkes/ npl/ Minden Pictures; (snake) David Hosking/ FLPA/ Minden Pictures;

FRONT MATTER
1 (macaw), Joel Sartore/ NationalGeographicStock.com; 1 (kangaroo), Christopher Meder/ Shutterstock; 1 (polar bear), FloridaStock/ Shutterstock; 1 (giant panda), Eric Isselée/ Shutterstock; 1 (gorilla), Eric Gevaert/ Shutterstock; 1 (chamois), George F. Mobley/ NationalGeographicStock.com; 1 (penguin), Konrad Wothe/ Minden Pictures/ NationalGeographicStock.com; 2 (polar bear), FloridaStock/ Shutterstock; 2 (macaw), Joel Sartore/ NationalGeographicStock.com; 2 (chamois), George F. Mobley/ NationalGeographicStock.com; 3 (giant panda), Eric Isselée/ Shutterstock; 3 (gorilla), Eric Gevaert/ Shutterstock; 3 (kangaroo), Christopher Meder/ Shutterstock; 3 (penguins), Konrad Wothe/ Minden Pictures/ NationalGeographicStock.com; 6 (top), Rich Lindie/ Shutterstock; 6 (center), Philippe Clement/ naturepl.com; 6 (bottom), Miriam Stein; 7 (top), Michael & Patricia Fogden/ Minden Pictures; 7 (center left), iStockphoto.com; 7 (center right), Chris Schenk/ Foto Natura/ Minden Pictures; 7 (bottom left), James P. Blair/ NationalGeographicStock.com;7 (bottom right), Pete Niesen/ Shutterstock

NORTH AMERICA
8-9, Joel Sartore/ NationalGeographicStock.com; 10 (top to bottom), iStockphoto.com; Rusty Dodson/ Shutterstock; dragon fang/ Shutterstock; Christophe Testi/ Shutterstock; FloridaStock/ Shutterstock; Tom Grundy/ Shutterstock; 11 (top to bottom), ND Johnston/ Shutterstock; iStockphoto.com; dragon fang/ Shutterstock; Tom Grundy/ Shutterstock; Dave Rodriguez/ iStockphoto.com; Christophe Testi/ Shutterstock; FloridaStock/ Shutterstock; 12-13, Mike Theiss/ NationalGeographicStock.com; 12 (top to bottom), Audrey Snider-Bell/ Shutterstock; Anton Foltin/ Shutterstock; Joel Sartore/ NationalGeographicStock.com; 13 (top to bottom), Sara Robinson/ Shutterstock; Jill Fromer/ iStockphoto.com; Tony Campbell/ Shutterstock; Ronald Berg/ iStockphoto.com; Eric Isselée/ Shutterstock; 14, Tom Walker/ Riser/ Getty Images; 15 (top), William Albert Allard/ NationalGeographicStock.com; 15 (bottom), Juniors Bildarchiv/ Alamy

SOUTH AMERICA
16-17, Pete Oxford/ naturepl.com; 18 (top to bottom), Steve Byland/ Shutterstock; Sedin/ Shutterstock; Eric Isselée/ iStockphoto.com; Christian Musat/ Shutterstock; Eric Isselée/ Shutterstock; Dr. Morley Read/ Shutterstock; 19 (top to bottom), Vivid Photo Visual/ Alamy; Steve Byland/ Shutterstock; Sedin/ Shutterstock; Eric Isselée/ iStockphoto.com; Christian Musat/ Shutterstock; Eric Isselée/ Shutterstock; Dr. Morley Read/ Shutterstock; 20-21, guentermanaus/ Shutterstock; 20 (top to bottom), Philip Dowell/ Dorling Kindersley; Dorling Kindersley/ Getty Images; Thomas Marent/ Minden Pictures; 21 (top to bottom), Ingo Arndt/ Minden Pictures/ NationalGeographicStock.com; Stephen Dalton/ Minden Pictures; Eric Isselée/ Shutterstock; Vladimir Wrangel/ Shutterstock; Eric Isselée/ iStockphoto.com; 22 (top), Mark Moffett/ NationalGeographicStock.com; 22 (bottom), Joel Sartore/ NationalGeographicStock.com; 23, Mark Moffett/ Minden Pictures

EUROPE
24-25, Dietmar Nill/ Foto Natura/ Minden Pictures/ NationalGeographicStock.com; 26 (top to bottom), George F. Mobley/ NationalGeographicStock.com; Dmitry Deshevykh/ iStockphoto.com; blickwinkel/ Alamy; Jose Durao/ NationalGeographicStock.com; Andy Gehrig/ .iStockphoto.com; 27 (top to bottom), Dietmar Nill/ Foto Natura/ Minden Pictures; George F. Mobley/ NationalGeographicStock.com; Dmitry Deshevykh/ iStockphoto.com; blickwinkel/Alamy; iStockphoto.com; Andy Gehrig/ iStockphoto.com; blickwinkel/ Alamy; 28-29, Roca/ Shutterstock; 28 (top to bottom), Jens Stolt/ Shutterstock; Reinhard Holzl/ imagebroker/ Alamy; Eric Isselée/ Shutterstock; 29 (top to bottom), Gertjan Hooijer/ iStockphoto.com; Shutterstock; Ziga Camernik/ Shutterstock; Bob Balestri/ iStockphoto.com; Wildlife GmbH/ Alamy; 30, Wil Meinderts/ Foto Natura/ Minden Pictures; 31 (top), Torsten Lorenz/ Shutterstock; 31 (bottom), Nicole Duplaix/ NationalGeographicStock.com

ASIA
32-33, Tom Brakefield/ Stockbyte/ Getty Images; 34 (top to bottom), Christine Gonsalves/ Shutterstock; Mark Bowler / NPL/ Minden Pictures; Eric Isselée/ iStockphoto.com; Konrad Wothe/ Minden Pictures; Eric Isselée/ Shutterstock; Mark Kostich/ iStockphoto.com; 35 (top to bottom), Eric Isselée/ Shutterstock; Christine Gonsalves/ Shutterstock; Konrad Wothe/ Minden Pictures; Eric Isselée/ iStockphoto.com; Eric Isselée/ Shutterstock; Mark Kostich/ iStockphoto.com; Mark Bowler / NPL/ Minden Pictures; 36-37, Peter Barker/ Panos Pictures; 36 (top to bottom), Eric Isselée/ Shutterstock; Jeff Banke/ Shutterstock; Joe Ferrer/ Shutterstock; 37 (top to bottom), Tui De Roy/ Minden Pictures; iStockphoto.com; Bogdan Boev/ Shutterstock; David Hosking / FLPA/ Minden Pictures; Roland Sietre/ SeaPics.com; 38 (both), Lisa & Mike Husar/ Team Husar; 39, Lisa & Mike Husar/ Team Husar

AFRICA
40-41, Mary Robbins/ NationalGeographicStock.com; 42 (top to bottom), Winfried Wisniewski/ Corbis; Eric Gevaert/ Shutterstock; Jeff Gynane/ Shutterstock; fivespots/ Shutterstock; Sam D Cruz/ Shutterstock; Eric Isselée/ Shutterstock; 43 (top to bottom), Eric Isselée/ Shutterstock; Eric Isselée/ Shutterstock; Eric Gevaert/ Shutterstock; Eric Isselée/ Shutterstock; Eric Isselée/ Shutterstock; fivespots/ Shutterstock; 44-45, enote/ Shutterstock; 44 (left to right), Chris Mattison/ FLPA/ Minden Pictures; Nadezhda Bolotina/ Shutterstock; Eric Isselée/ Shutterstock; 45 (top to bottom), Johan Swanepoel/ Shutterstock; Jason Prince/ Shutterstock; James Pierce/ Shutterstock; Eric Isselée/ Shutterstock; Mike Wilkes/ npl/ Minden Pictures; 46, Karl Ammann/ Digital Vision/ Getty Images; 47 (top), Jane Goodall/ NationalGeographicStock.com; 47 (bottom), Cyril Ruoso/ JH Editorial/ Minden Pictures/ NationalGeographicStock.com

AUSTRALIA
48-49, Mitsuaki Iwago/ Minden Pictures/ NationalGeographicStock.com; 50 (top to bottom), Neale Cousland/ Shutterstock; Susan Harris/ Shutterstock; Robyn Butler/ Shutterstock; Christopher Meder/ Shutterstock; Sandra Caldwell/ Shutterstock; Susan Flashman/ Shutterstock; 51 (top to bottom), Eric Isselée/ Shutterstock; Georgina Steytler/ iStockphoto.com; Christopher Meder/ Shutterstock; Sandra Caldwell/ Shutterstock; Susan Flashman/ Shutterstock; Neale Cousland/ Shutterstock; Robyn Butler/ Shutterstock; 52-53, Dropu/ Shutterstock; 52 (top to bottom), Brian Skerry/ NationalGeographicStock.com; David Doubilet/ NationalGeographicStock.com; Ian Scott/ iStockphoto.com; 53 (top to bottom), Four Oaks/ Shutterstock; Randy Olson/ NationalGeographicStock.com; Mike Parry/ Minden Pictures/ NationalGeographicStock.com; iStockphoto.com; Peter Kyne/ Shutterstock; 54 (top), Natphotos/ Photodisc/ Getty Images; 54 (bottom), Christopher Meder/ Shutterstock; 54, Deanna Markham/ NationalGeographicStock.com

ANTARCTICA
56-57, Tui De Roy/ Minden Pictures/ NationalGeographicStock.com; 58 (top to bottom), Rich Lindie/ Shutterstock; Flip Nicklin/ Minden Pictures; Flip De Nooyer/ Foto Natura/ Minden Pictures/ NationalGeographicStock.com; Paul Nicklen/ NationalGeographicStock.com; idreamphoto/ Shutterstock; Flip Nicklin/ Minden Pictures; 59 (top to bottom), Leksele/ Shutterstock; Paul Nicklen/ NationalGeographicStock.com; Flip Nicklin/ Minden Pictures; Flip De Nooyer/ Foto Natura/ Minden Pictures/ NationalGeographicStock.com; Jan Kratochvila/ Shutterstock; Rich Lindie/ Shutterstock; Flip Nicklin/ Minden Pictures; 60, Phillip Colla/ SeaPics.com; 61 (top), Richard Fitzer/ Shutterstock; 61 (bottom), Doug Perrine

Trade ISBN: 978-1-4263-0699-0
Library ISBN: 978-1-4263-0727-0

Printed in Hong Kong
10/THK/1